D1117419

THE CONDITIONED IMAGINATION FROM
SHAKESPEARE TO CONRAD

THE CONDITIONED IMAGINATION FROM SHAKESPEARE TO CONRAD

DISCARDED

Studies in the Exo-cultural Stereotype

Michael J. C. Echeruo

Professor of English Literature
University of Ibadan

 HOLMES & MEIER PUBLISHERS, INC.
IMPORT DIVISION
IUB Building
30 Irving Place, New York, N.Y. 10003

First published 1978 by
THE MACMILLAN PRESS LTD
London and Basingstoke
Associated companies in Delhi
Dublin Hong Kong Johannesburg Lagos
Melbourne New York Singapore Tokyo

Printed in Great Britain by
UNWIN BROTHERS LTD
Woking and London

British Library Cataloguing in Publication Data

Echeruo, Michael Joseph Chukwudalu
    The conditioned imagination
    1. English literature — History and criticism
    I. Title
    820'.9   PR401
    ISBN 0-333-22085-4

Contents

Preface

This study is in two parts. The first (chapter 1) is a general theoretical excursion on the problem of the 'exo-cultural stereotype', as I see it, and on what I hope will increasingly come to be formally recognised as an important element in criticism, namely, the 'conditioned imagination'. Chapters 2 to 5 (the second part) are case studies, selected not only because they help justify the preliminary theoretical discussion but also because they show in what significant ways the understanding of a work of literature can be affected by an awareness of these issues. In an ostensibly liberal age such as ours, it is only too tempting to misread the earlier literature of Europe by denying it the strength of the original prejudice or preconditioning which both influenced and supported it. My hope is that this book will help in at least preventing this.

I wish to thank the editors of *Shakespeare Quarterly*, *Southern Review* and *English Studies in Africa* for permission to reuse (in their now revised form) some of the material which first appeared in their journals.

Ibadan   M.J.C.E.
April 1977

Acknowledgements

The author and publishers wish to thank the following who have kindly given permission for the use of copyright material.

Curtis Brown Limited on behalf of the Estate of William Faulkner, and Random House Inc., for an extract from *Light in August*.

Jonathan Cape Limited on behalf of the Estate of Robert Frost for the poem 'Neither Out Far Nor In Deep', from *The Poetry of Robert Frost*, edited by Edward Connery Lathem.

A. P. Watt & Son on behalf of M. B. Yeats and Miss Ann Yeats, and Macmillan Publishing Company Inc., for 'On Hearing that the Students of our New University have joined the Agitation against Immoral Literature', from *The Collected Poems of W. B. Yeats*. Copyright 1912 and renewed 1940 by Bertha Georgie Yeats.

Withers, Solicitors, on behalf of the Trustees of the Joseph Conrad Estate, and Doubleday & Company Inc. for an extract from 'The Nigger of the *Narcissus*'.

We have made every effort to trace the copyright holders but if any have been inadvertently overlooked we will be pleased to make the necessary arrangements at the first opportunity.

1 The Conditioned Imagination

Literature is human utterance, formalised and structured. As utterance, literature is analogous to language itself in being based on a system of codes and registers and having an intrinsic grammar which is itself part of a system of conventions in the society or the culture to which it belongs. Hence, we know a literature the way we know a language, first by recognising its internal characteristics, and secondly by understanding the significance or 'meaning' which the speakers of the language attach to these characteristics. To speak of the structure of a sentence, Jonathan Culler says, is necessarily to imply an internalised grammar that gives it that structure. 'When a speaker of a language hears a phonetic sequence, he is able to give it meaning because he brings to the act of communication an amazing repertoire of conscious and unconscious knowledge.'[1] So, too, with literature. To have this repertoire of knowledge is to have what Culler calls 'literary competence'.

But Culler's discussion of the idea of competence is somehow limited to the literary quest *per se*, rather than to the specific non-literary conventions which, as it were, accompany the primary literary game. He says: 'In order to identify various levels of coherence and set them in relation to one another under the synoptic heading or theme of the literary quest one must have considerable experience of the conventions of reading poetry.'[2] F. R. Leavis phrases this differently. His own 'implicit assumption' that his judgement of a work of art is 'right' and 'universally valid', he says, 'has training behind it. . . . One that has entailed a complexity of

1

necessarily collaborative frequentation — a matter, most importantly, of exercising sensibility and responsive thought on the work of creative writers. Such a judgement seems to oneself a judgement of reality, and for arriving at it there are no rules, though there is active informing "principle".'[3]

The argument of this book goes further than both Culler's and Leavis's. I argue that in approaching a work of literature which involves what I later describe as an 'exo-cultural' character or theme, we need to take into account the influence of the 'culturally-conditioned imagination' of the audience on both the creation and realisation of a work of art, since the codes of such a work, like those of language itself, are 'articulated and structured, and their meaning depends upon the homology between their epistemological and their semiological systems'.[4] In other words, the literary event combines the conventions of the language of literature with the language of the culture; and just as a language is private to those who speak it (and serves, to that extent, to exclude non-speakers from the act of communication), so is the total meaning of a literary work in many ways defined and predetermined by the collective interpretation given it by its true and original audience. Accordingly, we say that the conventions of literature are not altogether literary in character. The judgement that Shakespeare's Falstaff is *the* 'mis-leader of youth', that Richard Cumberland's Napthali is 'an ugly little monkey with a broken accent'[5] or that William Faulkner's Dilsey (*The Sound and the Fury*) is 'the embodiment of Christian resignation and endurance' is not a specifically literary one. Each of these judgements presumes the existence of place, time and context; and as Irving Howe has said of Dilsey, 'whether time will do for [her] what it has done for Don Quixote, no one can say'.[6]

In his essay 'Of the Standard of Taste' (1757), David Hume tried to establish that it is impossible to be final in matters of literary taste. Taste, he argued, is determined by two factors: 'the different humours of particular men' and 'the particular manners of our age and country'. For an example of the first of these factors, Hume pointed to the variations of individual taste over time. 'At twenty Ovid may be the favourite author, Horace at forty, and perhaps Tacitus at fifty. Vainly would we, in such cases, endeavour to enter into the sentiments of others and divest ourselves of those propensities which are natural to us.' As to national and period preferences, Hume cited the case of comedy which is not easily transferred from one age or nation to another. 'A Frenchman or Englishman is not pleased with the *Andria* of Terence or *Clitia* of Machiavel.'[7] Hence, according to this argument, a people cannot but read and judge literature in the light of what may be called their particular historical and metaphysical situation.

This is hardly surprising since literature can be said to be part logical, part affective; or (in less refined terminology), part fact, part prejudice. This duality is clearly at the heart of many of the major issues in the theory of literature; for example, in the distinction frequently made between the 'communication of fact' in a literary work and its ability to give 'pleasure through some use of the inventive imagination'. This distinction assumes somehow that, in giving pleasure, a literary work — say, a novel — engages in some peculiar or idiosyncratic colouring of fact. This is usually granted as true of the satiric novel where the writer's point of view, and the targets of his satiric disposition, are more directly manifest. Referring specifically to Sinclair Lewis's *Babbitt* but with the larger context of the satiric novel in mind, Rebecca West once wrote:

To write satire is to perform a miracle. One must hate the world so much that one's hatred strikes sparks, but one must hate it only because it disappoints one's invincible love of it; one must write in denunciation of ugliness and put the thing down in unmistakable black and white, yet keep this, as all written things, within the sphere of beauty.[8]

To the extent that the hero of Lewis's novel is a recognisable Anglo-American type, the account of his career in the novel is, we should say, almost true-to-fact. The 'transports of exasperation' in the novel are, in Rebecca West's words, 'the Celt getting angry with the Englishman. For Zenith City and Babbitt are amazingly English. They represent that section of America which seems the least affected by the Latin and Jewish and Celtic leavens; the resemblance of kinship is patent, even blatant.'[9] Maxwell Geismar saw more than 'factual' truth in the novel. *Babbitt*, he says, is set in Hell: 'it is almost a perfectly conceived poetic vision of a perfectly. . . standardised material' — an opinion which Mark Schorer rather matter-of-factly took to mean that in *Babbitt*, 'nothing is either a lie or a truth'.

> . . . Lewis creates a visual world and a world of manners that appear to be absolutely solid, absolutely concrete; but all that accumulation of data has from the outset been made to submit too severely to selective strictures of two highly limited and limiting observations that what emerges in fact is an image and a criticism of middle-class society and not in the least a representation of it.[10]

Lewis's abstractions are ultimately successful because his civilisation is predisposed to accept as 'true' that novel's proposition (itself a 'half-truth', in Schorer's words), that Lewis's portraits represent the American Man and Mainstreet USA. 'I know the Babbitt type. . . every American city swarms with [Babbitt's] brothers. They run things in the Republic East, West, North and South. . . They are the palladiums of 100% Americanism.'[11]

One may find in this logical/affective duality partial

explanation for that other distinction between factual and poetic truth which derives from the idea that poetic truth is only truth in a context; that is, opinion made valid by the character of its artistic environment. How this validation is actually achieved is not easily established. It would seem, at least, to require that divinely-inspired madness which, in his *Phaedrus*, Plato says has to enter into the poet's 'delicate and virgin soul', in order there to 'inspire frenzy' and 'awaken lyrical and all other numbers'.[1 2] Such a compelling passion or madness would attract to itself an appropriate fable and style and so justify the poet's frenzy by the sheer force of a unifying vision. In the poetry of Wallace Stevens, for example, regarded by many critics as a Platonist,[1 3] the opposition between reality and imagination — between 'the lion in the lute' and 'lion locked in store' — is immediate and unequivocal, and only because his poetry has a philosophic and cerebral character does it manage not to surprise and intimidate us with its many assumptions, attitudes and preconceptions.

> I do not know which to prefer,
> The beauty of inflections
> Or the beauty of innuendoes.[1 4]

Even Romantic expressionism in its many manifestations can be seen as a variation of a kind on this primary distinction. The dilemma in which John Casey says 'English criticism since Wordsworth' is involved depends entirely on the notion that a poem is 'in some sense, the vehicle of the poet's feeling'.[1 5] 'Because English critical theory has been bound up with a (philosophical) terminology which assumes only a contingent connection between inner states and their outward expression,' Casey argues, it has not been able to solve the problem of the dichotomy between 'objective' and 'subjective'. Wordsworth's definition of poetry as the 'overflow of powerful feeling' was actually a rather generous one which could accommodate practically any utterance that is sufficiently strong and distinctive. Middleton Murry admits as much when he argued that 'the source of style is to be found in a strong and decisive original emotion... An individual way of feeling and seeing will compel an individual way of using language.'[1][6] Romantic expressionism, therefore, had to rely on the integrity and autonomy of the poet's feelings; his expression of his feelings is authentic only in so far as the expression appears to us as 'inevitable'; that is, as having satisfactorily 'named' the original feeling. 'The test of a true idiosyncrasy of style is that we should feel it to be necessary and inevitable: in it we should catch an immediate reference back to a whole mode of feeling that is consistent with itself.'[1][7] Because Wordsworth's poetry seeks to be all-embracing, to incorporate rather than exclude, it would be inexact to associate this generosity of heart with prejudice in the more pejorative sense of that word. Nevertheless, Wordsworth's views and attitudes are so thorough, strong and single-minded — even in his search for harmony and sincerity — that they can be said to amount to a kind of proper and responsible prejudice.

> Great God! I'd rather be
> A pagan suckled in a creed outworn,
> So might I, standing on this pleasant lea,
> Have glimpses that would make me less forlorn;
> Have sight of Proteus rising from the sea;
> Or hear old Triton blow his wreathed horn.

It would be true, then, to maintain that the importance, and even the seriousness, of a work of literature is directly a function of the force of the conditioning frenzy, or prejudice. Accordingly, it is necessary to argue that great literature *has to have* great prejudice to sustain it. Conversely, a work is not literature if it does not have a worthwhile prejudice to justify. We may phrase this differently and say that serious literature is essentially the statement *and* justification of human prejudice at the highest and most impersonal level. Literature takes human attitudes — high-minded as well as petty — and envelopes them in a new light which both reveals and deceives. It is the only way it has of giving vitality, plausibility and cogency to individual and communal interpretations of the phenomenon of life. Milton's *Paradise Lost* makes sense only in the context of the communal faith (or prejudice) which itself sustains every character, episode and phrase of that great work. The portraits of Satan in both Book II, (lines 1—10) and Book IV, (lines 34—5; 73—8), for example, depend entirely on our being acquainted with a shared predisposition with Milton by which act we are in a position to recognise the immensity of Milton's once-great angel whose grandeur, Milton says, outshone 'the wealth of Ormus and of Ind' and whose fall turned him into the 'miserable' angel 'at whose sight all the stars/Hide their diminished heads'.

At its subtlest level, prejudice manifests itself in literature as 'tone', 'irony' or 'sarcasm'. Robert Frost's 'Neither Out Far Nor In Deep' is a case in point.

> The people along the sand
> All turn and look one way.
> They turn their back on the land.
> They look at the sea all day.
>
> As long as it takes to pass
> A ship keeps raising its hull;
> The wetter ground like glass
> Reflects a standing gull.
>
> The land may vary more;
> But wherever the truth may be —
> The water comes ashore,
> And the people look at the sea.

They cannot look out far.
They cannot look in deep.
But when was that ever a bar
To any watch they keep?

Obviously, this way of looking at the human condition has
been formed by the experiences, attitudes and assumptions
which, for convenience, we describe as the poet's vision of
life. But though Frost's vision is certainly not the obvious or
even customary way of looking at the human condition, it
has been made plausible, acceptable and beautiful in the
poem by Frost's deliberately ambivalent pseudo-doubt, especially in the third stanza. Here, clearly, is one example of a
transformation of prejudice, a way of eliminating what may
be called the personal stake. We call it a transformation only
to emphasise that attitudes, whether privately held or com-
munally supported, are the foundation for literature and are
responsible ultimately for what we call its power, and
sometimes its beauty. Yeats's 'On Hearing that the Students
of our New University have joined the Agitation against
Immoral Literature' offers another example of this transformation of prejudice into art, this elimination of the
personal stake.

Where, where but here have Pride and Truth,
That long to give themselves for wage,
To shake their wicked sides at youth
Restraining reckless middle-age?

Here the complex feelings of scorn and anger which could,
indeed, have been given expression in other non-literary
ways, have been thoroughly transformed into the biting irony
of the poem's absurd contradictions. Yeats's attitudes to
youth, to literature, even to the moral and ethical integrity of
the university are the force behind his poem, but the explicit
nakedness of these attitudes has been covered over by the

stylisation of art. The result is the elegance which we admire.

These general theoretical questions are not the main subject of the present study but they are quite relevant to the problems of what we call the 'exo-cultural stereotype' and of the 'conditioned imagination' which creates and sustains it. There is a sense, of course, in which human nature is everywhere and always the same, and, in consequence of which, a work of art ought to be capable of eliciting the same responses from individuals, epochs and nations. Dr Johnson had such a possibility in mind when he claimed in his *Preface to Shakespeare* (1765) that 'Nothing can please many, and please long, but just representations of general nature. Particular manners, can be known to few, and therefore few only can judge how nearly they are copies.'[18] One may, therefore, conclude that Hume's 'sources of variation' notwithstanding, it is possible for readers to come to some agreement about the *basis* of our disagreements; to agree, for example, that it is possible, through a close and discriminating analysis, to show that what the forty-year-old enjoys is actually there in Horace. What we also have to accept is that (as semiologists tell us) human nature is itself like language in being a single system with several sub-systems or grammars. The logic is the same, but the programme is various. Hence, the meaning of poems, plays or novels within a language and a culture becomes the sum total of the programmes the particular culture adopts; and this meaning includes the culturally-sanctioned values attached to words and situations in any given literary work. Thus, the full meaning of Shakespeare's *Titus Andronicus* includes the total response of Shakespeare's culture to Titus and Aaron and to their predicament in the play. To read the play without an awareness of the possible function of Aaron's colour as a signal, for example, would be to eliminate the very collective imagination of the Elizabethan audience which gave meaning to such terms as 'moor', 'night hag', 'black sire' and 'young devilings'. And it would not matter for the purposes of this argument whether Shakespeare reinforces or undermines that primary and collective attitude; he would still be addressing himself to it. *Titus Andronicus* in other words, belongs to a particular civilisation, the same, in fact, that among other things, approved Canon Fifteen at the Council of Illiberis (A.D. 305) by which the marriage of Europeans with Jews and pagans came to be regarded as adultery. As long as English literature was 'private' to England, it, like the English language itself, inevitably belonged to the initiated. What needs doing, then, is a decoding of this literature in the light of the changed circumstances whereby literatures which were originally conceived of in tribal (*i.e.* national) contexts have now become international and cross-cultural.

It is true, indeed, as Nathanael Culverwell observed in *An Elegant and Learned Discourse on the light of Nature, with several other Treatises* that in a way, 'as face answers face, so does the heart of one man answer the heart of another, even the heart of an Athenian, the heart of an Indian'.[19] Yet, as is evident even from Culverwell's juxtaposition of *Indian* and *Athenian*, and his subsequent reference to the 'barbarous Scythian', 'wilde American', 'unpolisht Indian', 'superstitious Egyptian' and 'subtile Ethiopian', differences are known to exist the basis for which, to cite Hume again, is simply *prejudice*: that 'fourth unphilosophical species of probability. . . derived from *general rules*, which we rashly form to ourselves'.

An Irishman cannot have wit, and a Frenchman cannot have solidity; for which reason, though the conversation of the former in any instance be visibly very agreeable, and of the latter very judicious, we have entertained such a prejudice against them, that they must be dunces or fops in spite of sense and reason.[20]

These are, as it were, general introductory remarks. The four central essays of this book are concerned with prejudice

in a more specific sense than this. They are concerned with
that representation of life in literature which is shaped by a
conditioned imagination of both author and audience; that is,
an imagination already predisposed by habits and associations
to a particular view of what I call 'the exo-cultural phenomenon'.

Take Faulkner's short story, 'Red Leaves', for example. In
it, Faulkner records this conversation between two American
Indians. One of them claims that the flesh of the Negro has a
'bitter taste'.

> 'You have eaten it'?
> 'Once. I was young then, and more hardy in the appetite
> than now. Now it is different with me.'
> 'Yes. They are too valuable to eat now.'
> 'There is a bitter taste to the flesh which I do not like.'
> 'They are too valuable to eat, any way, when white men
> will give horses for them.'[2][1]

This is clearly an example of chilling Faulknerian comedy.
His two Indians are beautifully differentiated in their attitude
to the Negroes. One sees them as meat and rejects them for
the 'bitter taste to the flesh'. The other sees them simply as a
source of wealth, too valuable to eat when white slave owners
'will give horses for them'. But beyond the comedy, which is
universal, there is a specific problem of determining how to
judge these Indians as men. The problem arises, I suggest,
simply because the characters are Indian. In 1959, Faulkner
was asked if the Chickasaw Indians were ever known to be
cannibals.

> No, there's no record, but then it's — who's to say whether
> at some time one of them might not have tried what it
> tasted like? Quite often young boys will try things that
> they are horrified to remember later, just to see what it
> was like. . . Maybe as children they have found a dead man

and cooked some of him to see what he tasted like. But they were not cannibals as far as I know.[22]

Two points stand out in Faulkner's explanation. First is the attempt to relate the characterisation of the Indians to general human psychology, to what young boys will often do out of natural curiosity. The second is the suggestion implied in Faulkner's argument that it is permissible to speculate freely on what an Indian might do. The plausibility of this speculation does not depend, as in the first case, on general human psychology but on what Faulkner's culturally-determined imagination can consider possible in the necessarily different world of the American Indian. Accordingly, both a general and a peculiar view of the Indian survive in Faulkner's characterisation. The general view gives us readers the impression of fellow feeling and understanding; of experiencing the same sense of comedy that we would expect from all mankind. But the peculiar view of these Indians (the basis for which, quite significantly, is unstated in the short story) defines them in terms of a strange and unique moral and cultural environment. To this extent, it seriously qualifies the degree to which our initial sense of familiarity with these Indians can be justified.

We should therefore say of Faulkner's two Indian characters that they are not two individuals who happen to be Indian, but two figures whose personality has to be recognised from the outset as Indian. Faulkner's readers are neither required, nor expected, to make the same moral judgments about these Indians as they would of other people. Quite simply, these Indians have to be judged according to what Faulkner's explanation would encourage us to call an 'Indian psychology'. Hence, the psychology of the two men is for the greater part submerged in that of the group, of the tribe. The fact that they are American Indians becomes as important as, perhaps even more important than, the fact that they are men. It is in this sense that we describe them as stereotypes existing in a special exo-cultural context.

The term, exo-cultural stereotype, should perhaps be explained further. A stereotype, generally speaking, is a character who appears to us to have more of the features of a class than those of an individual. The braggart soldier, for example, manifests little more than those characteristics associated with that class of soldier. This kind of stereotype is a deliberate simplification of human character. It does not attempt the more subtle task of representing those nuances of character which alone establish the difference between the individual from the group to which he belongs. But because the braggart soldier or his equivalent is *part of his own culture*, the audience knows that he is a deliberate simplification or exaggeration.

This kind of stereotype differs from what I call the exo-cultural stereotype. Whereas in the case of the cultural stereotype detailed exploration of the character of the stereotype is also an exploration of the character of the audience, in the other case, there is no such identification. This is because it is almost impossible for the audience and the artist to see the character as other than *an example* of some other group to which the character belongs. Even when the artist succeeds in creating the illusion that his exo-cultural characters are 'rounded', this 'roundedness' is sustained by the concurring sensibility of the artist's culture, by the disposition of readers within his culture — his primary audience — to accept that representation of the character as possible and natural. The explanation for this is to be found in the fact that the exo-cultural character functions within a frame of attitudes created by a tradition outside his person. Because he is expected (not just thought) to be motivated differently, it becomes impossible to assimilate him completely into the artist's culture or to write about him other than as what he is to the artist's culture — a type. By concentrating on the broad features of the type rather than on the unique complexities of the individual, the reader or audience tries to understand the group through the individual character. In traditional literature — that is literature about characters within the culture — the reader tries to understand the individual; in the literature of the exo-cultural stereotype, he strives to understand the group through the individual.

This brings us back to what may quite justly be called cultural prejudice. For what emerges from the application of the concept of the exo-cultural stereotype to the study of national literatures is an awareness of the extent to which the imagination of the artist (as well, of course, as that of the audience) can be conditioned by cultural prejudices and attitudes; or, more relevantly, how great works of art can be produced under the impetus of some of the basest of prejudices. For this reason, we ought to distinguish private from communal prejudice which latter may be said to derive from the values and the theology of the whole culture. Because it is only against that background that he can make himself understood, it is to this communal prejudice that the artist addresses himself.

The problem is not a new one. In the *Inferno* (Book XXXIV), Dante describes one of the three faces of Satan in the following words: 'The left one was, to look at, such as those are Who come from where the Nile falls to its valley'.[2 3] The other two faces were 'vermilion' (for the Jew) and 'betwixt white and yellow' (for the Mohammedan Arab). This characterisation is dependent on the distinctions already established by the theological culture of Christian Europe. What the artist within the culture can do is simply to *use* these distinctions in the fashioning of his poetic utterance. There is, in this sense, nothing personal or private in Dante's prejudice against Jew, Arab or African. In fact, we should recognise that a writer's departure from the set attitudes of his culture does not necessarily indicate the disappearance of the cultural stereotype. Ben Jonson's *Masque of Blackness* praises the beauty of Ethiopian women because

> . . . in their black, the perfect'st beauty growes;
> Since the fix't colour of their curled haire,
> Which is the highest grace of dames most faire
> No cares, no age can change.[24]

But we must not therefore read that masque as the repudiation of the traditional attitude to the Negro colour. The fact remains that Ben Jonson's masque is a 'play' or a 'variation' on that attitude. The 'beauty' of the Ethiopian is still *sui generis* and Jonson's strategy in the Masque is to allow the debate to proceed long enough for him to take back all that praise of Blackness in the companion *Masque of Beauty*.

> Yeeld, Night, then to the light,
> As *Blackness* hath to *Beautie*;
> It was for Beauty, that the world was made.[25]

If this is understood, then the values implied or assumed in the representation of the exo-cultural stereotype in a given work become part of its essential background. Such values become an inescapable part of the work and have to be taken into full account in the appreciation of the work's meaning. If this is appreciated, then the representation of these culturally-determined values in literature will be ascertained by justly literary standards. It would not, then be simply a matter of the personal attitudes of the artist, as an individual, but of the particular slant or emphasis he begins with which have a predetermining effect on the interpretation of character as well as event. It was Blake, after all, the revolutionary, who wrote 'The Little Black Boy': 'My mother bore me in the southern wild,/And I am black, but oh! my soul is white.'[26] In explaining the poem, Whitesell claimed that this couplet 'is no apology but merely a way of saying that externally (physically) he is black but internally (spiritually) he is white. The temptation to equate blackness with ignorance and sin, in contradistinction to whiteness as a symbol of purity and innocence, must be carefully shunned.'[27] This argument has obvious weaknesses, as another critic has pointed out.

> If we deny 'white' the implication of 'purity and innocence' at this point, the whole line becomes meaningless; yet if we grant this implication, the line does become an 'apology'. It seems to me that the poem requires here something quite different from line 2. To be consistent with the central image, the black soul should say (in effect, though more poetically!): 'And I am black, but O! my soul is beyond all distinctions of colour.' Blake's failure to write what his own basic metaphor calls for — his disruptive use, instead of 'white' and 'black', as trite provincial symbols — wounds the poem.[28]

The problem is neither with the poem nor with Blake, but with the conditioned imagination which finds it impossible to allow the manipulation of the basic metaphors which Blake attempts. Beyond this, we have the other problem that Blake himself is seeking to express himself through a subversion of existing symbolic equivalencies. Nevertheless, Blake could not (it is impossible to) pretend that the established and traditional correspondencies do not exist; for this reason his praise of the black boy could not have been phrased differently. Blake was saying exactly what Desdemona, in absolute sincerity, had said of Othello: 'I saw Othello's visage in his mind'.

This preconditioning of the response of the writer's audience to the phenomenon of an exo-cultural stereotype has important consequences. Faulkner's *Light in August* is a great novel of undeniable power and graphic clarity. Yet these qualities have not, somehow, availed much in giving specificity to the character of Joe Christmas, the novel's hero. The problem is, actually, similar to that which we will see in reading *Othello*. What Othello was to the Elizabethans, Joe

Christmas is to Faulkner's America. As with Shakespeare, so with Faulkner. And their greatness as artists is in that ability to give authenticity and complexity to attitudes which are, essentially, founded on prejudice; the ability to characterise the intricacies of a powerful communal attitude to the fascinating but disturbing exo-cultural phenomenon. Just as some critics have tried to deny the blackness of Othello, so have others tried to argue that Joe Christmas is not black. The fact of the denial is itself proof that Joe Christmas's colour (whether white, black or in-between) is a crucial element in the story and that without that element, and the prejudices associated with it, Faulkner's story would, in fact, be quite pointless.

An easy way out of the difficulty is to argue that Joe Christmas is *not* the American Negro, nor the mulatto, but the modern man: 'a modern tragic protagonist', as John Lewis Longley Jr, has called him. By this he meant that Joe Christmas is

> one who is typical of the age and not so remote from the typical human beings to make emotional identification difficult for the spectator. . . . The modern hero must typify the major myths and major problems of our century. In a cosmos where all is chaos and all standards have disappeared, he will very likely be destroyed as a result of his failure to define himself correctly in relation to that cosmos.[29]

Behind this argument is a supposition that it was Faulkner's intention (or the effect of his novel) to present 'a violent chaotic and absurd' cosmos in which a Joe Christmas would be a typical man and a possible hero.[30] Such an assumption is patently false and the falsity is implied in the often-quoted observation that Joe Christmas's tragedy was that he didn't know what he was and would never know,[31] — which is to say that he certainly wasn't white but did not know it. Joe

Christmas could never become a typical modern hero in the large sense proposed by Longley and others because he is, literally, a non-descript whose predicament derives not so much from what he thinks or does, but from what he is, or (to phrase this more exactly) from what he is thought to be. For only such a clarification of the argument can explain Richard Chase's grand remark that Faulkner 'made some attempt at modernising [Joe Christmas] by making him in effect a Conradian or post-romantic existentialist hero'.[32] This is clearly not the case. Joe Christmas is neither the modern man nor the post-romantic existentialist but a creation of white American culture: both the fictional hero and his real-life analogues derive their being from the attitude of a culture that sees them as exo-cultural stereotypes.

Because Faulkner's critics do not quite realise this, they do not see how unsatisfactory is the argument which every 'liberal' critic now wants to restate: that Joe Christmas is neither white nor black. Cleanth Brooks, for example, speaks condescendingly of those commentators who refer to Joe Christmas's 'mixed blood', and speaks rather of Joe Christmas's 'alleged' Negro blood. He concludes: 'Joe does not know what he is. Throughout his life, he lashes out at both the white community and the Negro community. But the warping of his mind and spirit. . . is the result of the way in which he has been reared from infancy. The biological matter is quite irrelevant.'[33] Brooks is quite wrong. The biological matter is supremely relevant as far as the community and novel are concerned. Why else all the detailed attempt at reconstructing Christmas's ancestry? The predicament of Joe Christmas is simply that of a man who cannot be called white because he is somehow also black and *has to be called* black because he is not white. But why should a mulatto be called black and not white? The answer in fact is to be found in that communal attitude which regards Joe Christmas's black ancestry as a diminution of the sacred purity of his white blood. The so-called tragic mulatto was the creation of a racial attitude which assumes that whiteness redeems while blackness condemns. In short, it was implied that the mulatto (as a special sub-species of the nigger) had a tragic dimension to his being. If he had been all nigger, perhaps he would have lived and died a simple nigger; instead, Joe Christmas had the privilege of white blood. Joe Christmas is, accordingly, not a Negro in the ordinary sense of the word but a misbegotten child of the American South, at once white and black, and *therefore* (as Faulkner clearly states) necessarily torn between civilisation and savagery.

> But his blood would not be quiet, let him save it. It would not be either one or the other and let his body save itself. Because the black blood drove him first to the negro cabin. And then the white blood drove him out of there, as it was the black blood which snatched up the pistol and the white blood which would not let him fire it. And it was the white blood which sent him to the minister, which rising in him for the last and final time and sent him against all reason and all reality, into the embrace of a chimera. . . Then I believe that the white blood deserted him for the moment. . . It was the black blood which swept him by his own desire beyond the aid of any man, swept him up into that ecstasy out of a black jungle where life has already ceased before the heart stops and death is desire and fulfilment.[3 4]

And when he is killed, he is purged of his degrading black blood.

> . . . and from out the slashed garments about his lips and loins the pent black blood seemed to rush like a released breath. It seemed to rush out of his pale body like the rush of sparks from a rising rocket; upon that black blast the man seemed to rise soaring into their memories forever and ever.[3 5]

In the event, he became a tragic wreck, impelled by two necessarily incompatible but intrinsic urges. Faulkner's remark, therefore, that Joe Christmas didn't know what he was and would never know is true in a sense the critics have not appreciated. It is not *who* Joe Christmas is — a matter of identity — that is the question, but *what* he is — an ontological question.

The surprise, really, is that a contrary opinion could be entertained. Faulkner was, after all, part of the naturalist school of American novelists whose origins can be traced back to Crane or at least to Frank Norris and Sherwood Anderson. That school, to the extent that it derived part of its inspiration from Zola and the French naturalists, sought to represent the effect of 'compulsive and deterministic' forces on human conduct. *MacTeague* (1899) has been described by one critic as 'an exaggerated, melodramatic example of so-called naturalistic fiction'.[36] It nevertheless was a powerful and responsible attempt at the exploration of human character. That MacTeague should deteriorate under the influence of animal spirits may sound ridiculous, but that does not change the argument of the novel; nor does it alter the fact that the explanation which the novel offers for the hero's character is based on this influence and on no other. In other words, *MacTeague* seeks to illustrate the effect of one *kind* of compulsion on a character in precisely the same way that *Light in August* seeks to show the effect of another kind of compulsion on the principal character.

So, too, with Sherwood Anderson's *Winesburg, Ohio* (1919), where again some primal forces are said not only to influence the relationships between the hero and the community, but in fact to determine what the character of the hero himself is going to be. In effect, the novel gives expression to bold and far-reaching statements about human nature. What the novel establishes — or tries to establish — is a theory of character based on the view of man as a purposeless and irrational being whose conduct is determined by instinct and self-will. It may be argued, of course, that Anderson did not succeed in fully establishing this theory because it was not, in fact, possible to believe in it. Nevertheless, it would be true to say that in *Winesburg, Ohio*, as well as in his *Poor White* (1920), Anderson was attempting to domesticate naturalism on the American soil by locating the impetus to destruction in his provincial or urban characters and dooming them, from the start, to puzzled, unheroic but tragic careers. It would seem right to conclude that both Norris and Anderson were doing what Stephen Crane and the French naturalists before them had done: find some fundamental impulse to destruction in their heroes and document the inevitable process of deterioration and tragedy. The nature of these impulses may differ from one author to another. In *Maggie: A Girl of the Streets* (1893), for example, Crane speaks of the chemistry of human psychology; Anderson speaks of sex as a necessary and a predetermining life-force. In Faulkner's *Light in August*, it is blood not sex or chemistry that is the predominating influence. An important difference worth bearing in mind, however, is the fact that Faulkner's novel approaches the status of a national (or at least a regional) epic to an extent that the works of Crane and Anderson never could. In Faulkner, we have the sense of the deliberate and calculated unfolding of a simple yet profound story which has significance for men and nations — for the destiny of peoples. We should recognise this difference and relate it (as is proper) to the essential Calvinism of Faulkner's thought and of his South. It is this Calvinism that transforms his otherwise simple naturalistic novel of race and sex into an epic tale of history and destiny. It is this combination of late Victorian naturalism and orthodox Southern Calvinism that brings philosophy and theology together in the novel, and thereby turns a frankly regional (or should we say, local-colour) novel into an epic novel of the South, a novel to answer such ultimate questions as, 'where did we sin?' and 'how can we be saved?' These, certainly, are the questions posed by Faulkner's novels, and especially by *Light in August* and *Go Down, Moses.*

In this connection, we recall the argument of 'Delta Autumn', especially of the tent scene when the negro girl accuses Isaac McCaslin of ruining Roth: 'You spoiled him,' she says to Ike, 'when you gave to his grandfather that land which didn't belong to him, not even half of it by will or even law.'[37] That land was secured through greed and exploitation and it stood as a curse on the McCaslin clan. It could never really be theirs in any proper sense and so would lead the McCaslins to a certain degradation as was, in fact, already evident in Roth's illegitimate child by Jim's daughter. In any event, this original sin associated with the appropriation of land, prepares us for the true tragedy of the American South, as Faulkner saw it. The old man Ike had, in fact, mistaken Jim's daughter for a white woman and only realised his error when she referred to her aunt's taking in some washing to help cover their expenses. The shock of this realisation affected Ike profoundly. He cried out 'in a voice of amazement, pity, and courage . . . cried again in that thin nor loud and grieving voice . . . his voice began to rise again but he stopped it'; he spoke 'harshly, rapidly, but not so harsh now and soon not harsh at all but just rapid.'[38] Ike's agitation is the result of his vision of a degraded Delta. Jim's daughter — this being that was truly neither white nor black — was one form which the curse on the land was going to take. His vision of the future is that of an American where 'Chinese and African and Ayran and Jew all breed and spawn together until no man has time to say which one is which nor cares.'[39] It is, therefore, out of a prophet's sense of anguish and hope that Isaac tells the Negro girl to 'go back north. Marry: a man in your own race.'[40] In the context of *Go Down, Moses*, Isaac McCaslin's message is quite clear and Faulkner's sense of the doom on the Delta is unmistakable.[41] It is this same sense of doom that provides the background for *Light in August*. 'Delta Autumn' concerned itself with the land and the white masters; *Light in August* with the new brood spawned in a doomed Delta. Put simply the novel is about one of that brood who illustrates in himself and in his relation to society Faulkner's view of the tragic possibilities of what the novel calls 'the black shadow in the shape of a cross'.[42] Joe Christmas needs, therefore, to be seen as an exo-cultural stereotype — a character given plausibility by the conditioned imagination of the alien culture in which he is obliged to perform. He is the creation of the group imagination and survives as a plausible being for as long as this imagination can sustain him.[43]

This specific conclusion in respect of Faulkner's fiction is, however, not as important as the acceptance of the underlying argument of this chapter that prejudice is not incompatible with literary merit and that, in respect of the exo-cultural stereotype, such prejudice is, in fact, a condition for literary merit. In the chapters that follow, I intend to examine in some detail four major applications of this general argument in order to demonstrate the possibility of and necessity for a new critical approach based on the twin notions of the exo-cultural stereotype and the conditioned imagination.

2 Shylock and the Conditioned Imagination

In an article in the Quartercentenary issue of *Shakespeare Quarterly*, Irving Ribner argues that when comparisons are made between *The Merchant of Venice* and *The Jew of Malta*

> and it is perhaps inevitable that they should be — it is usually with the assumption that Shakespeare imitated Marlowe. To some we have Shakespeare palliating the antisemitism of Marlowe with a more sympathetic portrait of a Jew; to others we have Shakespeare striving to outdo Marlowe in antisemitism by presenting a more sympathetic view of the Christian world than Marlowe's.[1]

Ribner further argues that the 'proposition' that *The Jew of Malta* 'exerted much influence' upon *The Merchant of Venice* is 'questionable' and 'can be positively neither denied nor affirmed'. He feels, also, that the propositions that Shylock 'owes much to Barabas', and that 'Shakespeare is indebted to Marlowe for "much of the atmosphere of his Jewish theme" ' are 'dubious propositions at best'. If these two plays are to be compared, he concludes, 'it must not be for what we learn about the influence of one dramatist upon the other, but for the insight such comparison may afford into the vast gulf which divides the two major Elizabethan dramatists' (p. 45).

But surely the gulf is not that vast, and the aim of such comparisons should not be simply to defeat the argument for Marlowe's influence on Shakespeare. Its aim should instead be to appreciate the (perhaps independent) effect of an antecedent tradition on two nearly contemporary dramatists;

to lead us to an awareness of its scope and tenacity and to enable us to understand whatever else these dramatists may have wanted, each in his own way, to do either with or to that tradition. In that case, the specific influence of Marlowe (or of *Il Pecorone*) on Shakespeare will not be crucial to the understanding of any parallel situations in Shakespeare and Marlowe. More specifically, even if the parallels in plot and emphases between Marlowe's and Shakespeare's play do not establish an influence one on the other, they would at least suggest that certain plot-situations and emphases were quite susceptible in Elizabethan times to the kind of specific treatment accorded them by the two major dramatists.

Even then, another issue needs to be resolved. It is the problem of the Jew as stereotype and its place in the criticism of Elizabethan drama. The problem arises the moment we try to understand a comment such as George Duthie's, that 'in the *Il Pecorone* story the Jew is a conventional figure. Shakespeare vitalises the character.'[2] But then, compared to Shakespeare's play, Ser Giovanni's story is a mere anecdote. It is certainly not about the Jew as such, but about the many trials of the main character, Giannetto. What Giovanni takes entirely for granted in his story, Shakespeare had to spell out and elaborate on in his play. Moreover Ser Giovanni manages to give us the background of Venetian law against which to see the Jew's otherwise incredible obstinacy. 'The question [of the Jew's demands] was much debated, and every one said that the Jew was in the wrong, but since Venice had a reputation as a place of strict justice, and the Jew's case was legal and formally made out, nobody dared to deny him, but only to plead with him.'[3] Hence in keeping with this tradition of strict justice, the Jew, on his defeat, is not even allowed the ten thousand ducats he was now willing to accept: 'If you want your pound of flesh, take it. If not, I shall declare your bond null and void. . . Everyone present was delighted and they all mocked at the Jew, saying, "He who lays snares for others is caught himself". The Jew, seeing that he could not do what he had wished, took his bond and tore it in pieces in a rage' (p. 474). This is the Jew of *Il Pecorone*, and he is in essence as realistic or as conventional as Shakespeare's Shylock.

Perhaps this question is related to yet another. Ribner does draw our attention to two opposed statements by C. J. Sisson and H. B. Charlton. According to Sisson, 'the Jews in London had the immense comfort of communal life, undisturbed, with full freedom to carry on their trades and professions, and even the further solace of the regular practice of religious rites in the home, even if in secret. The Jewish problem was, in truth, no problem in the reign of Elizabeth.'[4] That is to say, *The Merchant of Venice* has nothing to do with the Jewish question. Charlton, for his part, claims that 'about 1594, public sentiment in England was roused to an outbreak of traditional Jew-baiting; and for good and evil, Shakespeare the man was like his fellows. He planned a *Merchant of Venice* to let the Jew dog have it, and thereby to gratify his own patriotic pride of race.'[5] In other words, the play is Shakespeare's contribution to the contemporary anti-Semitic movement. Both declarations are quite relevant to the problem of reconstructing the forces acting on the imagination of the audience and the dramatist in their understanding of the play. But the crucial evidence to look for is not the local or topical momentum that gave immediacy to the plays but, possibly, the latent folk memory which could be induced by a dramatist to a suspension of its own belief or disbelief in Jewish cruelty and blasphemy.

It should not be really surprising that this should be so if we remember that critics who will describe Barabas of Marlowe's *The Jew of Malta* as a 'monster' will, however, argue that although the hero of *Tamburlaine* is presented in the same extravagant Marlovian view, he cannot properly be called monstrous. For such readers, the fact that Tamburlaine is a *Scythian* is considered immaterial to his character and to the tragedy. The reason for this distinction is fairly clear. In

Tamburlaine, Marlowe uses the fact of his hero's Scythian origins only to create a conflict of a theological kind between the hero's world and that of Christian Europe. The Elizabethan audience cannot see Tamburlaine as an immediate or local problem, and the issues which develop in the play do not need to reflect such popular or parochial sentiments as confound *Othello* and *The Merchant of Venice*.

Tamburlaine does, nevertheless, make assumptions. The hero's ruthlessness belongs to the hero both as an individual and as a Scythian. But in the play, Marlowe's interest is not to explore but to *present* him and, in that process, certain ideas and arguments. *The Jew of Malta*, unlike *Tamburlaine*, is about an alien in a Christian world. Unlike Tamburlaine, Barabas had a very immediate implication for the world in which he is being presented. That is, the emotions of the audience are more directly and more immediately involved in *The Jew of Malta* than in *Tamburlaine*, because the issues that arise for Malta have a greater practical and topical relevance than those in *Tamburlaine*. We may then say, speaking generally, that *Tamburlaine* is Romance where *The Jew of Malta* is Life. It is this framework of the Romance that has saves Tamburlaine from the kind of close scrutiny visited very often on Barabas.

Even so, the 'atheism' which Tamburlaine champions on Marlowe's behalf is his own stereotypal 'cause'. That is to say, it is not only in the language of Tamburlaine's denunciation of the gods that his atheism resides but also, not surprisingly, in the fact that a godless Scythian shepherd is the play's exalted hero. By choosing this kind and class of hero, by endowing him with the power and the grandeur of his poetry, and especially by making him the spiritual-minded lover of Zenocrate, Marlowe was thereby subverting all the established expectations of the audience. By definition, Marlowe's reversal of expectations constituted an insult to the values of the Christian world for, though Marlowe is not championing Tamburlaine's cause, as such, he is prepared to use him as a scourge on the comfortable orthodoxy of his own world. The Scythian hero ('the barbarous Scythian/Or he that makes his generation messes/To gorge his appetite', as *King Lear* describes the kind) was ideally suited, both by classical and Christian specifications to represent Marlowe's atheistic attitudes. And his audience would have had no difficulty in believing it of Tamburlaine.

Marlowe's manner is, thus, the same in the treatment of Barabas as in that of Tamburlaine: only the conditions under which the two characters appear differ. Both characters are Marlowe's way of celebrating the *heroic impossible*: the villainous exuberance of Barabas is the equivalent of the godless magnificence of Tamburlaine. But, significantly, these celebrations are attempted, not by a denial of the traditional attributes of their types, but by a confirmation of them. Thus Barabas claims in II. i. 1—6:

> Thus, like the sad presaging raven, that tolls
> The sick man's passport in her hollow beak,
> And in the shadow of the silent night
> Doth shake contagion from her sable wings,
> Vex'd and tormented runs poor Barabas
> With fatal curses towards these Christians.

The speech ends where we could expect it to — with an opposition of Jew and Christian. If this ending were peculiar to Marlowe, we would have had to credit him with some unusually acute insight into what has come to be called ghetto-mentality. But since the motif is common enough in the literature about the Jew of Elizabethan and earlier times, we have reason to conclude that the sentiments attending it are also part of an unvarying store of Elizabethan expectations.

When we fail to take this communal or archetypal conditioning into account, we become liable to possibly sentimental readings of *The Merchant of Venice*. We are likely then to resort to the kind of over-statement we find in Grebanier's study of the play and in Ribner's essay. Shylock, Grebanier says, 'is not only a Jew; he is also a prototype of the banker, and what Shakespeare has to say on that head applies equally to Christian, Jew or Moslem.'[6] Ribner says of Shylock and Jessica that they are 'saved by the reality of love'. The 'highest reflection in terms of human love of God's divine love for man is the kind of love reflected in. . . Jessica's readiness to leave her father and his gold for Christian salvation'. These interpretations are misleading. In *The Jew of Malta*, Marlowe was unchristian enough (as Ribner points out in another context)[7] to expose the money-minded logic behind the Christian gesture of love through conversion. Ribner makes very much of this gesture: 'The punishment which Shylock at the end receives is his reception into the Christian community. . . Shakespeare's Jew comes at last to generate love in spite of himself and in this is some victory' (p. 48). But even a brief consideration of the Proclamation in *The Jew of Malta* will reveal the base motivation behind such offers of salvation through conversion to Christianity. 'First, the tribute-money of the Turks shall be levied against the Jews, and each of them to pay one-half of his estate. . . Secondly, he that denies to pay, shall straight become a Christian.' The third clause of the Proclamation suggests the calculating and cynical wickedness of the entire procedure: 'he that denies this, shall absolutely lose all.'[8] When in *The Merchant of Venice*, IV. i, the defeated Shylock 'accepts' the conditions imposed upon him by the court — 'Send the deed after me,/And I will sign it' — he is recognising the weight of Christian authority and submitting to it. The process is certainly not a 'reception' into the Christian community.

The reference to a 'reception into the Christian community' does, in fact, draw our attention to what may be considered the central pattern in Shakespeare's handling of his subject, namely, the elaboration of the Christian—Jew dichotomy. Or more specifically the conflict between Christian Europe and a Jew who was thought to be not only an usurer but also (by definition) a hater of Christ and of Christians.[9] To understand this conflict, it is necessary to appreciate the fact that from the start European prejudice against Jews was Christian and theological rather than racial in origin. The Church did have its early struggles with Judaism, but it was not until the ascendancy of Christianity as a state religion under the Emperor Constantine that the Christians had an opportunity to legislate effectively against Jews and Judaism. The destruction of Jerusalem had scattered the Jews all over the Roman Empire, where they were initially granted some protection. This toleration — of which the Constitution of Caracalla (A.D. 198–217) was an example — was repudiated through Christian pressure in the Theodosian Code. Among other things, this Code designated Jews as '*inferiores*' and '*perversi*', and regarded Judaism as a godless and dangerous sect ('*secta nefaria*', '*feralis*'). It also declared the meetings of Jews '*sacrilegi coetus*'.[10] Under Canon Fifteen of the Council of Illiberis (A.D. 305), marriages of Christians to Jews, pagans, or heretics were regarded as akin to adultery.[11] By an earlier edict of A.D. 423, marriages between Jews and Christians were made punishable by death.[12]

It is important that we insist on the religious foundation for this prejudice. Thus, though the Bishop of Caesarea objected to the Jewish rite of circumcision because he considered it a disgrace, he condemned it principally because he thought it was a heresy.[13] Naturally, there was difficulty in distinguishing between the social characteristics which differentiated Jews from Europeans and the doctrinal or ritual ones which separated Jews from Christians. Ephraem Syrus, for example, called the Jews 'circumcised vagabonds', and Ambrose, Bishop of Milan (A.D. 340–97), described the Synagogue in Mesopotamia as 'a house of depravity in which Christ is daily blasphemed'. Pope Gregory the Great declared the Jewish religion 'superstition, depravity and faithlessness'. And Thomas Aquinas was able to assert that the Jews were 'doomed to perpetual servitude and the lords of the earth may use their goods as their own'.[14]

The enthusiasm of these bishops in their hostility to Jews did not come from personal prejudice, but from strong religious attitudes deriving from theological convictions. St Isidore, for example, believed that the Jews were responsible for their suffering. In his *De Fidei Catholica ex veteri et novo Testamento contra Judaeis*, he declared that the Jews who killed Christ brought damnation on their posterity: 'Judaei posteritatem suam damnaverunt.'[15] St Isidore depended for his justifying text on Matt. xxvi: 25: 'His blood be upon us and upon our children'. He quotes this passage several times through his writings, even linking it with the curse of Noah and Cham. Just as Cham, through his derision of his father's nakedness, had brought about the curse on his children, 'sicut et plebs Judaei, quae Dominum crucifixit etiam in filiis poenam damnationis suae transmisit' (LXXXVII, 237). In his *Allegoriae Quaedam Sacre Scriptura*, he elaborates further on this comparison. Cham, he claims, stands for the Jews, 'quo Christum incarnatum atque mortuum derident'. He continues: 'Chanaan, filius ejus, qui pro patrio delicto maledictione damnatur [Gen. ix], posteritatem indicat Judaeorum, qui in passione Domini damnationis sententiam exceperunt, clamantibus Judaeis: Sanguis eius super nos, et super filios nostros.'[16] In all his attacks on the Jews, it would thus appear, St Isidore was motivated by the blasphemy of the Jews on Christ, from which the analogies with the Cham episode gain considerable force.[17]

It is essentially this tradition of the hatred and irreverence of the Jews towards Christ which was carried over through the early Church into the Renaissance. The Jew was thus identified as a reject, as an inveterate hater of Christ and Christians. In medieval drama, the Jew is shown consistently in this role. Though the New Testament made it clear that

Christ was scourged and tormented by Roman soldiers,[18] the *Play of Corpus Christi* (1415) has four Jews accusing Christ, four persecuting him, and others compelling him to bear the cross.[19]

Along with this tradition of the Jew as a hater of Christ was another of him as the usurer. This tradition can be traced back to the biblical stories of the publican and of Christ's cleansing of the Temple. Especially, it was associated with Judas's betrayal of Christ for thirty pieces of silver. The cycle of mystery plays acted at York on Corpus Christi Day during the fourteenth and fifteenth centuries gives numerous examples of this. 'Judas, like the bargaining usurer, asks for thirty pence saying that he would like to "make the merchandise"; he grumbles when the Romans fail to hand the money over at once. He is also described as Christ's treasurer in which office he had shown his "Jewish" instincts by converting ten per cent of the money to his own use, a fact which receives special emphasis in the play.'[20] Money-lending for interest was of course considered immoral and unnatural in the Old Testament[21] and even in classical antiquity,[22] though, for obvious reasons, many people engaged in it. The early Church condemned lending at a profit and claimed that the ruling of the Mosaic Law against what was called 'usury among brothers' amounted to a universal interdiction against the taking of any interest under any circumstances. St Ambrose made an allowance for Christians dealing with Jews and Mohammedans, arguing that it was no crime to take interest from a religious enemy: 'From him exact usury whom it would be no crime to kill'.[23] By the end of the twelfth century, however, Christian money-lenders were so numerous that the Church had to reaffirm its stand. The Second Lateran Council (A.D. 1139) declared the unrepentant usurer condemned by the Old and New Law alike and therefore 'unworthy of Christian burial'.[24] The *Quod Super Nonullis* Bull of 1258 by Pope Alexander IV went so far as to make the taking of interest an act of heresy.[25]

These restrictions on banking, which many Christians found onerous,[26] made the Jews (who were not subject to these laws but were resident within the Christian community)[27] the one group of people who could engage in the necessary and lucrative trade without the force of the Inquisition being brought to bear on them.[28] The Christians who did engage in the business were regarded as lost souls, as Dante specifically states in the *Inferno* (Cantos XI and XVII). The result was naturally a despised minority made rich and powerful by the religious decisions of a Christian Europe. Hence, for example, Barabas's boast in *The Jew of Malta*: 'Rather had I, a Jew, to be hated thus,/Than pitied in a Christian poverty.' This boast was, of course, Marlowe's way of projecting into his drama the sentiment which a disgruntled Christian audience would imagine to be most natural to a Jew. As Marlowe makes Barabas assert, the riches of the Jewish merchant 'are the blessings promised to the Jews./And herein was old Abraham's happiness'.[29]

This ambivalent response to Jewish prosperity is also to be found in Shakespeare's play, particularly in Shylock's retelling of the story of Jacob and Laban's sheep in which Shylock claims to be emulating Jacob's practice. Laban's story became well-known especially after the Reformation, when the emphasis on Old Testament stories became general. In the dramatisations of the story, Esau is the villain, Jacob the hero. Shylock appears to be defending his usury by ironically recalling the fact that in medieval plays, Jacob's otherwise dishonest scheming was justified and praised.[30]

Also connected with the tradition of Jewish usury is the Lorenzo-Jessica sub-plot in the play. The abduction of the Jewish maiden (her father's heir) and the robbery of her father (with or without her connivance) were stock Renaissance *exempla*.[31] Shakespeare creates his characters within that tradition.[32] In V. i. 14–17, Lorenzo repeats the seduction motif, leaving Antonio to supply the robbery motif by forcing Shylock to endow the couple with half his fortune.[3][3]

When, therefore, we speak of stereotypes in a play such as *The Merchant of Venice* or *The Jew of Malta*, we are really thinking of that complex product of an imagination conditioned by the expectations of its audience, that product of an imagination which may modify or even reject the implications of its characterisation but cannot avoid addressing itself to those implications. Shylock is such a stereotype. He is introduced in the play specifically as a Jew stereotype. His conversation with Bassanio (I. iii. 1—34) is dominated by the overriding interest in money ('Three thousand ducats, well') and his intense hatred for Christians: 'Yes, to smell pork, to eat of the habitation which your prophet Nazarite conjured the devil into: I will buy with you, sell with you, talk with you, walk with you and so following: but I will not eat with you, drink with you, nor pray with you'. The blasphemous reference to Christ could not have gone unnoticed and unappreciated in Christian Elizabethan England. The effect of this blasphemy and this usuriousness is further heightened by Shylock's self-confessed reasons for hating Antonio. They are reasons, in fact, which place Shylock irrevocably in the tradition of the anti-Christ and the inveterate usurer.

> I hate him for he is a Christian
> But more[3][4] for that in low simplicity
> He lends out money gratis, and brings down
> The rate of usance here with us in Venice.
> (I. iii. 37—40)

The fact that this hatred and this usuriousness are self-confessed suddenly gives a certain plausibility to what was, all along, a conventional assumption. Shylock does not become an individual because he gives expression to this confession, but because of our disposition to believe the dramatic convention of a confession as affirming our experience of that kind of character. If, for example, Shylock had denied these characteristics, he would have then seemed to us an idealised and unrealistic characterisation, a sentimental representation of the Jew.[35]

In III. i., Shakespeare allows Shylock his spirited and persuasive speech complaining of the inhuman treatment he has received at the hands of the Christians, and in effect, asserting that he, too, is as mortal a man as the Christian. The speech has been used frequently to justify a reading of the play as representing Shakespeare's plea for a humane treatment of Jews. It is a speech, according to J. Dover Wilson, which makes Shylock 'entirely more human than the conventional Jew of *Il Pecorone* or than the magniloquent monster created by Marlowe.'[36] On the other hand, Allan Bloom, who describes Shylock's speech as 'an appeal to the universality of humanity', finds that Shylock 'includes only things which belong to the body' in his list of characteristics on which he bases his claim to equality with his Christian tormentors. 'What he finds in common between Christian and Jew is essentially what all animals have in common. The only spiritual element in the list is revenge.'[37]

To be properly understood, the speech has to be seen first as the culmination of the Jew—Christian contrast begun by Salerio a few lines earlier. Shylock had called Jessica his 'own flesh and blood. . . I say my daughter is my flesh and my blood'. Salerio's retort is definite: 'There is more difference between thy flesh and hers than between jet and ivory' (III. i. 31, 33, 34—5). This contrast between Shylock and Jessica, the true Jew and the convertite, is pressed further in Shylock's speech. Shylock is thus not really pleading for compassion; he is justifying his determination to revenge. Antonio, he argues, had no other reason for scorning and mocking him than that he is a Jew. From this premise, Shylock derives the major thrust of his argument:

Hath not a Jew eyes? hath not a Jew hands, organs, dimensions, senses, affections, passions? fed with the same

food, hurt with the same weapons, subject to the same
diseases, healed by the same means, warmed and cooled by
the same winter and summer as a Christian is? If you prick
us do we not bleed? If you tickle us do we not laugh? If
you poison us do we not die? and if you wrong us shall we
not revenge? — If we are like you in the rest, we will
resemble you in that. If a Jew wrong a Christian, what is
his humility? revenge! If a Christian wrong a Jew, what
should his sufferance be by Christian example? — why
revenge! The villainy you teach me I will execute and it
shall go hard but I will better the instruction. (III. i.
52–66)

Thus Shylock works himself into commitment to revenge by
establishing both the irrational and the hypocritical nature of
Christian humility and sufferance.[38] It is this argument that
Shylock has devised to answer Salerio's anti-Jewish jibes.

Sal.   Why I am sure if he [Antonio] forfeit, thou wilt not
take his flesh — what's that good for?[39]
Shy. To bait fish withal — if it will feed nothing else, it
will feed my revenge; he hath disgrac'd me... (III. i.
45–9).

Having thus understood Shylock's argument, we have to
recognise a second point, namely that the meaning of 'Jew' in
Shylock's speech is unspecified. Shylock takes 'Jew' here in
its most non-pejorative or neutral sense. Elsewhere in the
play, however, the name is consistently used in a disparaging
sense. In most cases, it is actually used to represent usuriousness, blasphemousness, and unkindness.[40] In such circumstances 'to hate a Jew' would, by definition, mean to hate a
covetous and uncharitable anti-Christ. Sigurd Burckhardt was
quite right in claiming that the rhetorical thrust of Shylock's
quarrel with Antonio forces our sympathies to go to the Jew
at that point: 'Shylock gets more than his share of good

lines. . . Shylock is powerful in his vindictiveness. . . Antonio is grandiloquent.'⁴ ¹ But this is not the complete story. The speech is in no way a denial of the grounds on which hatred of the Jew was established in the first place — his self-confessed hatred of Christ (and Christians) and his unbridled usury. For as long, therefore, as 'Jew' meant 'anti-Christ and usurer', Shylock's speech (like that of Edmund in *King Lear* or Caliban in *The Tempest*) cannot carry any justification *in itself.*⁴ ² European persecution of the Jews was not based on the belief that Jews were not capable of feeling pain. The pathos of Shylock's statement would in all certainty, then, be absorbed as a genuine but irrelevant protest, an evasion of the major issues in dispute. For the major conflict arises from the very fact of Shylock's Jewishness which made it all too certain that he would be the 'stony adversary, an inhuman wretch,/Uncapable of pity, void, and empty/From any dram of mercy', as the Duke himself describes Shylock (IV. i. 4—6).

The trial scene (IV. i) is an incomparable dramatisation of these stock attitudes. The setting is a court of justice in Venice. But the Duke is apparently there to plead for mercy rather than give judgment in justice. 'I have heard', Antonio tells the Duke, 'Your grace had ta'en great pains to qualify His rigorous course' (IV. i. 6—8). In his principal address to Shylock, the Duke reinforces the case for mercy in a peculiarly 'Christian' manner. The world, he says, expects mercy from 'this fashion of thy malice', and 'thy strange apparent cruelty'. Such a gesture of mercy would be expected even from the 'brassy bosoms and rough hearts of flint' of 'stubborn Turks and Tartars never trained to offices of tender courtesy'. In a deliberately malicious pun, the Duke in effect, asks from Shylock an un-Jewish virtue: mercy. 'We all expect a gentle answer, Jew' (IV. i. 31—4).

That Shakespeare and his audience could not have expected mercy from Shylock we can surmise not only from the Duke's unfair pun on a 'gentle' (meaning a 'gentile') answer, but from the consistency of Shylock's own reply. Not only has he sworn by 'our Holy Sabbath' against mercy, he would rather 'let the danger light/Upon your charter and your city's freedom', than yield. Shylock then reverts to the argument of his speech in II. i. and follows what he had judged to be the irrational nature of traditional Jew— Christian hostility. This time, however, he is willing to attribute his harshness to a whim. 'But say it is my humour, — is it answered?' (IV. i. 36, 38, 43).[43] Or more specifically we should call it a Jewish and anti-Christian whim, as Shylock himself describes it ('a lodg'd hate, and a certain loathing I bear Antonio'). Antonio confirms this: 'than which what's harder? — His Jewish heart'.

The harshness of these remarks should not, however, lead us to forget that *The Merchant of Venice* is a comedy and that, therefore, the trial scene is also, in essence, comic. It is a kind of comedy (Ben Jonson's *Volpone* is another example) where the high seriousness of the legal charge is reduced by the relative inconsequence of the punishment imposed. In *The Merchant of Venice*, moreover, the comedy of Portia's strategy in the court scene is of the same kind as the comedy of the casket scenes. In both cases, Portia has a rigged court which oddly enough is also a 'just' court. The essence of the comedy in both instances is in the double surprise — first, in the fear that the deserving party will lose his case through the meticulous justice of Portia's judgement, and, secondly, in the happy defeat of the worldly or unchristian antagonist. In the trial scene, Portia is the defender of her love and her faith. The disguise hides this fact from both Shylock and Antonio and thereby enhances the suspense. She grants Shylock's legal right to exact his bond; she demands and gets a confession from Antonio of his liability. But she uses all this to impose on Shylock an obligation of mercy: 'Then must the Jew be merciful'.

Portia's speech on the quality of mercy is a set speech designed to win Antonio back from the clutches of a

'heartless' Jew.[44] Shakespeare prepares for this speech by
establishing the pathos of Antonio's Christian resignation to
his 'unchristian' enemy: 'I do oppose my patience to his fury,
and am arm'd/To suffer with a quietness of spirit,/The very
tyranny and rage of his' (IV. i. 10–13). By introducing Portia
and her speech on Mercy, and by ensuring that Shylock
rejects her appeal, Shakespeare, as it were, makes a conventional dramatisation of a European stock-attitude seem very
human indeed. The conflict between Shylock and Antonio
accordingly becomes one between a Christian merchant —
forgiving and godly — and a Jewish merchant — unforgiving
and brutish. A Christian merchant was expected to yield to
Portia's appeal. As is borne out by the pattern of such Jew-
Christian confrontations since the Middle Ages, Shylock was
not expected to yield.

> Ainsi nous voyons, que le rapport entre le Juif et le
> Chrétien, est celui du Mal et du Bien, du temporel et du
> spirituel. Le Chrétien est doué de toutes les qualités, le
> Juif — de tous les defauts ... Le Chrétien est altruiste,
> généreux; le Juif — égoiste, cupide. Le bourgeois Chrétien
> n'est guidé que par l'amour de Dieu, le Juif — par l'amour
> de l'or.[45]

Portia adds another dimension to this stock dramatisation.
She links the plea for mercy with the threat of damnation.
Shylock's willingness to forgive would, in other words, also
secure salvation for him.

> therefore, Jew
> Though justice be thy plea, consider this,
> That in the course of justice, none of us
> Should see salvation ... (IV. i. 193–6)

Thus Shylock's 'Daniel come to judgement' is also (perhaps,
primarily) a partisan on the side of authority, the 'protector

of the King', as her assumed name of Balthazar implies. The consequent outwitting of Shylock at his own game ('I crave the law') accordingly becomes a double victory for Portia: it enables her to achieve her personal objective of freeing her husband's friend and allows her to establish a clear superiority of Christian over Jew, love and mercy over hatred and justice. The entire suspense depends on the audience being disturbed at the possibility of Christian Antonio being made over to the ruthless Jew. The comedy is in the disappointment of this possibility, in the victory of Christian over Jew.

It is interesting, from this point of view, to note the emphasis placed on Shylock's Jewishness after his rejection of Portia's plea. In the rest of the trial scene, Shylock is addressed by his name on only three occasions, but fifteen times as 'the Jew'. The five references to 'Christian' in this part of the scene are intended as contrasts to 'Jew'.[46] This particular contrasting of Shylock and Antonio is itself part of a larger statement concerning the false and the true religion. For Antonio represents the true Christian blend of justice and mercy. As the 'just' man, he asks Shylock to bestow the income of half his fortune on Jessica and Lorenzo. As the 'merciful' man, he demands that Shylock becomes a Christian. This demand, in fact, is both punishment[47] and (to the Christian conscience) kindness.[48] For conversion — the acceptance of Christ — had implications which were closely associated with the very basis of anti-Jewishness. Conversion, then, was the only kind of assurance of future goodwill which a Jew could give or which would be acceptable to the Christian imagination. In other words, conversion was not required of Shylock because he was a 'wicked' man but because he was a Jew. For a 'good' Jew also needed conversion, as one of Boccaccio's stories shows. Jehannot, the Christian,

> had particular friendship for a very rich Jew called Abraham, who was also a merchant and a very honest man and

trusty man, and seeing the latter's worth and loyalty, it
began to irk him some that the soul of so worthy and
discreet and good a man should go to perdition for default
of faith; wherefore he fell to beseeching him on friendly
wise to leave errors of the Jewish faith and turn to the
Christian verity. . . . [He] raised him from the sacred fount
and named him Giovanni. . . . and thenceforth was a good
man of a worthy and one of a devout life.[49]

The offer of conversion to Shylock was partly based on this
tradition and on the other tradition of hypocrisy which we
saw manifested in the Proclamation in *The Jew of Malta*.

Shylock does not accept the offer; he merely succumbs to
the pressure: I am not well, — send the deed after me,/And I
will sign it (IV. i. 392—3). The distinction comes out quite
clearly in Jessica, who combines the examples of Boccaccio's
Giovanni and Marlowe's Abigail and ceases to be a Jew. 'I
shall be sav'd by my husband, — he hath made me a Christian' (III. v. 17—18). It is the holy nature of her rejection of
father and faith, symbolised in the marriage with Lorenzo,
that makes her so endearing to the Christian imagination and
so endowed with all the tenderness of a lady of Romance.[50]

The revival of the Shylock debate in the quatercentenary
issue of the *Shakespeare Quarterly* is a reminder to us that
the theoretical resolution of the interpretation of a kind of
character like Shylock has not yet been attempted. Some
critics who want to be anti-Jewish will read the play as if the
fact of Shylock's usury and mercilessness is proof of Jewish
unkindness. Others, who think Shakespeare was above prejudice, see the play as a kind of defence of the man. Both
groups of critics tend to a conclusion for which there is no
justification: that powerful literature is not possible to an
author who shares the strong positive prejudices of his
civilisation. The problem of Shylock's characterisation is one
peculiar to a character-type which develops such great
permanence in alien culture that it is no longer possible to

differentiate the individual from the stereotype in him. Today, Shylock is not seen in the light of the conditioned Christian European imagination which originally celebrated him, but rather in terms of recent concepts of race prejudice and of the problems of minorities. Shakespeare's Shylock was addressed to a specific English audience. The creation of a Jew who did not have the characteristics of either Marlowe's Barabas or Shakespeare's Shylock, a Jew who did not serve as a comment on the accumulated religious prejudgements of the Christian conscience, would have required the reconditioning of the total experience of the contemporary culture. Thus, however human Shylock may seem — in the sense that he is subject to pain, humiliation and revenge — he remains a Jew, usurious and bitterly anti-Christian.

It is certainly not an accident that there are no unconverted good Jews in Elizabethan drama. Jew-baiting in such a community was not a mark of prejudice, if by the word we mean a response which is private, whimsical, malicious in intent, and resented by the community. Indeed, such baiting was often thought honourable and high-minded. Quoting Cyrillus and agreeing with him, Sir Walter Raleigh maintained that 'Cain and Abel were figures of Christ, and of the Jews: . . . as Cain after that he had slaine Abel unjustly, he had thence-forth not certaine abiding in the World: so the Jewes, after they had crucified the Sonne of God, became Runnegates: and it is true, that the Jews had neuer since any certaine Estate, Commonweale, or Prince of their owne vpon the Earth.'[5][1] So also in the Epistle Dedicatory to the English translation of Mornay's *The Trewnesse of the Christian Religion* (1587), Golding contends that

If any atheist Infidel or Jew having read this his work with aduisement, shall yet denye the Christian Religion to be the true and only pathway to eternal felicitie, and all other Religions to bee mere vanitie, and wickedness; must needs show himself vtterly voyd of humaine sense, or els obstinatly and wilfully bent to impugne the manifest truth against the continuall testimonie of his own conscience.[52]

Such was the sense of conviction and the temper of the Christian mind for which Shakespeare wrote. To understand the Jew in Elizabethan drama, we have to seek to recreate that attitude to what must have seemed 'a very terrible and powerful alien, endowed with all the resources of wealth and unencumbered by any Christian scruples.'[53]

Shylock was before everything else a non-Christian, a Jew. *The Merchant of Venice* is a comedy written for an Elizabethan audience about a Jew. All the terms count.

3 The Context of Othello's Tragedy

That Shakespeare meant the hero of *Othello*[1] to be a black man we can now take to be fairly established.[2] Important productions of the play can now assume without much explanation that Othello was a very black man indeed. Such an assumption naturally affects interpretation and emphasis. It provides us with a context for the tragedy. That context is the subject of this chapter.

It is perhaps necessary to remind ourselves that the reacceptance of a black Othello is a fairly recent one. It used to be argued, for example, that Shakespeare nowhere calls Othello an 'Ethiopian' or a 'Negro' as (it is thought) he would have done if he had intended his hero to be recognised as a black man. The word 'Moor', it was also argued, was invariably used in Elizabethan times to refer to Arabs of North Africa rather than to the negroes of the South. Moreover, the argument went on, Othello speaks of returning to Mauritania, meaning his home country of Morocco or Algiers. This would make Othello a 'tawny' instead of a 'Black' Moor. It was even argued that Othello claims to come from a royal family – an absurd claim, apparently, if he was really black, since most of the Africans in Europe at this time were ordinary soldiers of fortune, or else plain slaves. Kittredge sums up this line of reasoning by declaring that Othello was a 'Moorish noble of royal lineage ... Shakespeare conceives him as an oriental'.[3]

There have been arguments of a different kind tending to the same conclusion. Coleridge is said to have maintained that 'as we are constituted, and most surely as an English audience was disposed in the beginning of the seventeenth century, it would be something mysterious to conceive this beautiful Venetian girl falling in love with a veritable Negro. It would argue a disproportionateness, or want of balance, in Desdemona which Shakespeare does not appear to have in the least contemplated.'[4] Henry Reed followed this up with a demand that we 'clear the fancy of this false conception of Othello's colour, most of all for the sake of our sympathies with the gentle Desdemona'.

> ... for if we are brought to believe that this bright, this fairfaced Venetian lady was wedded to a black, we should almost be tempted to think that the monstrous alliance was fitly blotted out in its fearful catastrophe.[5]

Both arguments are based on the strong feeling that a black Othello would jeopardise the tragic effect of the play by alienating the sympathies of the audience. Or rather that the fine proportions of the play's actions and sentiments would be dislocated by the intrusion of a suggestion of miscegenation. The tragedy that results from the love of a gentle Desdemona and a black Othello, it is felt, would not really be tragic in the normal sense. It would be merely irresponsible and unfortunate. Miss Mary Preston accordingly dismissed the idea: 'We may regard, then, the daub of black upon Othello's portrait as an *ebullition* of fancy; a freak of imagination, — the visionary conception of a ideal figure, — one of the few erroneous strokes of the great master's brush, the *single* blemish on a faultless work. Othello was a white man.'[6]

The facts of the case should be clearly restated. In the first place, the tradition of the theatre, at least from Restoration times until the time of Kean, was to have a jet black Othello. 'This tradition', Bradley points out, 'goes back to the Restoration, and it almost settles our question. For it is impossible that the colour of the original Othello should have been forgotten so soon after Shakespeare's time, and most improbable that it would have been changed from brown to black.' His argument is supported by the discovery of an early illustration of *Titus Andronicus* which represents Aaron, the Moor of that play, with absolutely black face and hands. Shakespeare nowhere refers to Aaron as either 'Ethiopian' or 'Negro', and the illustration shows that Aaron was regarded as a black man. In the words of E. K. Chambers, the drawing 'may inform students of *Othello* as well as of *Titus* that to the Elizabethan mind a Moor was not tawny but dead black.'[7]

This, too, is something of an overstatement since the term 'Moor' was also used to describe Moors who were not black. We know, however, that the Elizabethans distinguished between 'white Moors' or Arabs, and Negroes or 'blackamoors'. The word 'blackamoor' is found as early as 1547 and 1548, and was used specifically of black men or Negroes, as they were called. John Pory's translation of *A Geographical Historie of Africa* by Leo Africanus confirmed this usage by making a consistent distinction between 'white or tawnie Moores', and 'Negroes or black-Moores'. This distinction is also found in Jonson's *Masque of Blackness* (1605) where the Ethiopian women are referred to as 'black-moores', or Negroes.[8] In *The Historie of the World* (1614), Raleigh consistently speaks of the 'Negro or Black-Moore'.

The word 'Negro' seems, moreover, not to have been very much in use at this time. Jonson, writing after *Othello*, says of the Ethiopians that they 'were called "Nigritae", now "Negroes": and are the blackest people of the world,' using the word as if it were the vulgar and recent form of a more correct Latin original. The census returns for some London parishes taken probably between 1558 and 1560 have references to Negro men and women living in the city. Yet one Clara among them is described as 'a Negra', while another (probably Jesse) is called 'a Negro'.[9] This distinction between masculine and feminine forms of the word would suggest that the word was only just coming into prominent popular use. We should therefore not be surprised that Shakespeare does not use it for his two black Moors, Aaron and Othello. Shakespeare used the word 'Negro' only once in his entire corpus. On that occasion, significantly enough, he made it equivalent to Moor. Launcelot is teased by Lorenzo in *The Merchant of Venice* (Arden edn. 1955, III. v. 34—6): 'I shall answer that better to the commonwealth than you can the getting up of the Negro's belly: the Moor is with child by you, Launcelot.' It seems clear from this evidence, and from the numerous references in the play to Othello as 'an old black ram', 'black Othello', and from the description of his appearance — his 'thick lips' and 'sooty bosom', for example — that the tradition of a black Othello was well-founded, and that Shakespeare intended it.

The other arguments that a black Othello, even if it was Shakespeare's decision, would destroy the true tragic effect of the play raise some quite important issues of relevance to the problems of the exo-cultural stereotype and the conditioned imagination. They suggest that an audience strongly enough conditioned against the blackness of Othello will find it impossible to accept the implications of the play's structure and rhetoric. Some critics have sought to counter this prejudice by speaking of Shakespeare's being more broad-minded and more humane than his audience. In making his Othello undeniably black, Philip Butcher says, 'and in giving this black man heroic stature quite in disagreement with the literary and social practice of his time, in making him profoundly human in his strengths and weaknesses, Shakespeare reveals both the quality and extent of his genius.'[10] Dover Wilson had, in fact, argued the same case, though from a very personal point of view. Only those 'who have not read

the play at all', he argued, 'could suppose that Shakespeare
shared the prejudice, inasmuch as Othello is his noblest
soldier and he obviously exerted himself to represent him as a
spirit of the rarest quality'. He recalled his experience of the
play when the role of Othello was played by Paul Robeson:

> I felt I was seeing the tragedy for the first time, not merely
> because of Robeson's acting. . . but because the fact that
> he was a Negro seemed to floodlight the whole drama.
> Everything was slightly different from what I had pre-
> viously imagined. . . the performance convinced me in
> short that a Negro Othello *is essential to the full under-*
> *standing of the play* [my italics].

Dover Wilson does not attempt to account in detail for this
feeling towards a Negro Othello, being content to record
some of the impressions he was left with after Robeson's
performance. He found Robeson's Othello 'primitive yet
dignified', and felt that this combination was responsible for
'the mingled tenderness and the ferocity of the murder scene
and the priest-like attitude in which he addressed himself to
the sacrifice'. 'Never shall I forget the radiant bliss of
Robeson's face as Othello first greeted Desdemona at Cyprus
or its dreadful deformation when he became possessed with
the "green-eyed monster".'[1][1]

These sentiments are obviously genuine; but they need to
be given critical or theoretical validity by being related to the
traditions within which Shakespeare worked and to the
differences in the mode of characterisation which the distinc-
tiveness of these traditions brings about. An attempt will be
made, therefore, to show how Othello's blackness affects the
play in material ways. It will be shown not only that
Shakespeare's Othello conforms more or less to the stock
Elizabethan notions of the Moor, but that this fact qualifies
the usefulness of recent attempts at a symbolic or Christian
reading of the play.

The character of Othello may be said to derive from three Elizabethan traditions of the Negro stereotype. According to one tradition which depends on contemporary ideas of the relationship of climate to psychology and character, people from the hot climates were thought to be particularly prone to the vices of jealousy, superstitiousness, lustfulness and cruelty.[1][2] This tradition did not, of course, exclude northern peoples from these vices. It only made it seem particularly appropriate for a character from the tropics to be said to be dominated by one or more of these humours. Aaron, in *Titus Andronicus* (ed. by A. M. Witherspoon, Yale, 1926), was such a tropical stereotype, and remained popular for years. Though he is simple-hearted, he is lustful in the extreme (as his affair with Tamora shows); he is cynical in his attitude to the defilement of Lavinia, cruel in his murders, and without conscience in his exultation in both:

> Tut! I have done a thousand dreadful things
> As willingly as one would kill a fly,
> And nothing grieves me heartily indeed
> But that I cannot do ten thousand more.
>
> (V. i. 141–4)

Eleazar, the Moor of *Lust's Dominion*, belongs to the same tradition, and his actions are guided by greed and lust, and are realised in innumerable murders. This lustfulness is a trait which even carries over to the women of the tropics. Zanthia, in *The Knight of Malta*, is an instance of the raven-coloured strumpet — lustful and irreligious. As she says of herself, 'I am full of pleasure in the touch'.[1][3]

We say that Othello belongs to this same tradition in the sense that his character is interpreted in relation to the elements of this stereotype. His enemies associate him with the Aaron-type; his defenders insist that his nobility lies in his difference from Aaron. He himself recalls the traditional view of the Moor type. He speaks of the 'vices of my blood'

(I. iii. 123) in his address to the Senate. Brabantio accuses him of 'stealing', abusing and corrupting his daughter. Roderigo arouses Brabantio's wrath by telling him that a 'knave of common hire, a gondolier' had transported Desdemona to the 'gross clasps of a lascivious Moor' (I. i. 125—6). Iago speaks of Othello as a lustful, 'an old black ram/. . . tupping your white ewe' (I. i. 88—9), and suspects him later of having affairs with his Emilia.

> For that I do suspect the lustful Moor
> Hath leap'd into my seat, the thought whereof
> Doth like a poisonous mineral gnaw my inwards,
>   (II. i. 290—2)

When Desdemona boldly insists on accompanying Othello to the wars rather than stay behind 'a moth of peace, and he go to the war', she is likely to be suspected of an improper forwardness: hence her speech,

> That I did love the Moor, to live with him,
> My downright violence, and scorn of fortunes
> May trumpet to the world: . . .
> I saw Othello's visage in his mind,
> And to his honours, and his valiant parts
> Did I may soul and fortunes consecrate:
>   (I. iii. 248—50, 252—4)

In this speech, though there is some (surely) unintended sexual punning in the reference to Othello's 'valiant parts', she shows herself to be aware of the pattern of her nation's thoughts, but declares herself free of any improper lustfulness by preaching a high-minded and radical personal virtue. But the sentiments thus expressed do not amount to proof, just as the lyrical language of Tamora's wooing of Aaron in *Titus Andronicus* did not constitute defence enough either:

My lovely Aaron, wherefore look'st thou sad,
When everything doth make a gleeful boast?
The birds chant melody on every bush,
The snake lies rolled in the cheerful sun,
The green leaves quiver with the cooling wind,
And make a chequer'd shadow on the ground.
Under their sweet shade, Aaron, let us sit . . .
(II. iii. 10—16)

This love song could not make her love for Aaron 'beautiful' because, as Lavinia put it, Tamora through her association with the Moor had become 'Semiramis, — nay, barbarous Tamora/For no name fits thy nature but thy own' (II. iii. 118—19). Hence, in *Othello*, Desdemona's plea to be with Othello has to be taken along with Othello's own self-deprecating explanation of his action in asking to take Desdemona with him to Cyprus.

I therefore beg it not
To please the palate of my appetite,
Nor to comply with heat, the young affects
In my defunct, and proper satisfaction,
But to be free and bounteous of her mind.
(I. iii. 261—5)

In an oath which closes this speech, he pledges not to let his 'disports corrupt and taint [his] business' in Cyprus (I. iii. 271). In his speech to the Senate, Brabantio had described Desdemona as

A maiden never bold of spirit,
So still and quiet, that her motion
Blush'd at her self: and she, in spite of nature,
Of years, of country, credit, everything,
To fall in love with what she fear'd to look on?
(I. iii. 94—8)

She was so modest, 'So opposite to marriage, that she shunn'd/The wealthy curled darlings of our nation' (I. ii. 67—8). But through the influence of Othello — or of some 'practices of cunning hell' (I. iii. 102) — she had become the changed woman who would '(to incur a general mock)/Run from her guardage to the sooty bosom/Of such a thing' as Othello (I. ii. 69—71).

But implied in Desdemona's pleas and in Othello's denials is a notion of the corrupting influence of the Moor on the virtue of Desdemona; and these scenes seek to save both characters from those very conclusions which would have come easily and naturally to an already conditioned imagination. The effect, then, of Othello's and Desdemona's speeches on 'continence' and marital 'rights' is to save Othello from the predictable charge of Moorish lustfulness and thereby also establish him as a fit subject for Desdemona's love since this particular weakness would have thus been shown to be absent *in Othello's case*. The scene thus also 'redeems' Desdemona's love by allowing us to see that Othello is not another Aaron desiring (in Aaron's words) 'to wanton with this queen,/This goddess, this Semiramis, this nymph' (*Titus Andronicus*, II. i. 21—2). Othello is heroic in the first place because he proves himself unlike the typical Moor of the Elizabethan stage. But he had to prove himself so. That proof by explicit denial was a necessary step towards his becoming acceptable to the imagination of the original audience of the play *Othello*.

As with his 'lustfulness' so also with Othello's credulousness and jealousy — both deriving from Elizabethan assumptions about the Moor stereotype. 'Their wits', Leo Africanus wrote, 'are but meane, and they are so credulous, that they will believe matters impossible which are told them.'[1][4] Iago is very much aware of these characteristics. The Moor, he says, is of

. . . a free and open nature too,

That thinks men honest that but seem to be so:
And will as tenderly be led by the nose . . .
As asses are. (I. iii. 397—400)

With this knowledge, Iago decides to take the advantage to exploit Othello's Moorish 'credulousness'. Because the imagination of the audience is already disposed to *expect* Othello to be credulous, Othello's plight is seen as truly pathetic, and Iago's conduct as devilish and unfair.

It is to this natural gullibility that Emilia alludes when she calls Othello 'thou dull Moor' in V. ii. 226. Othello confesses to it, too, when he compares himself to the 'base Indian' that 'threw a pearl away,/Richer than all his tribe'. If we recall the contempt with which the American Indian was regarded in contemporary Europe for his inability to value gold and jewels at their 'proper' worth,[15] we then understand better why Othello's explanation is likely to win him the genuine sympathy of the Elizabethan audience. For Othello's nobility — it is, as in all such cases, an individual exception — is shown as being undermined by an almost congenital intellectual weakness. Othello is, if you like, almost suffering from a racial (or national) defect.[16] Ironically it is precisely because Othello's gullibility is thought to be of this kind that his appeal seems to us tragic rather than merely sad. It is the only kind of sympathy due to an exo-cultural stereotype.

Similarly, Othello's jealousy is thought to be an inherited racial trait. Indeed, two modern critics, Dover Wilson and Paul Jorgensen, appear to think so too. 'The point,' Dover Wilson says, 'is that the trustfulness and simplicity, which Bradley, among others, notes as Othello's, seem his by nature when he is played by a Negro with all the winning integrity of that race.' And Jorgensen adds: 'It is also significant that besides his addiction to know, Othello's vocabulary for his own mental activity suggests emotional rather than intellectual apprehension.'[17] Though Iago's skill in tempting Othello is considerable, there has always been the feeling that

Othello gives in to the temptation too early. Rymer, for example, held that Othello laboured to be deceived by the suggestion of infidelity. More recently, it has been argued that Othello's fear of humiliation and his deep inner doubt that Desdemona would love anyone as unworthy as himself explain his eagerness to welcome I̲a̲g̲o̲'̲s̲ ̲i̲n̲s̲i̲n̲u̲a̲t̲i̲o̲n̲s̲ and to extend his sexual jealousy.[18] These arguments become irrelevant when we also see Othello as an Elizabethan Moor, and therefore as one belonging to a type which was thought exceptionally susceptible to jealousy; and to a civilisation that was very particular about the 'honesty' of its women. That, at least, was the impression left by Purchas and Hakluyt, and especially by Leo Africanus: 'No Nation in the World is so subject unto Jealousie, for they will rather lose their lives, then put up any disgrace in the behalf of their women.'[19]

That the Elizabethans saw the temptation of Othello as an unfair exploitation of a natural weakness, and felt it, for that reason, to be especially moving as tragedy, we can perhaps infer from that funeral elegy to Burbage which says that his 'chiefest part' in which 'beyond the rest he moved the heart' was that of Othello. But the deception in *Othello* is unique, and should not therefore be compared to Mephistopheles'. Unlike Goethe's devil, Iago is a great mind exploiting a child-like intellect. Where Faust acts from an almost divine romantic *lust*, Othello responds to Iago's temptation with a credulousness which is virtually pathological, yet connatural to him by his type. Two different processes are thus involved.[20] The resulting credulousness is not, moreover, what F. R. Leavis says it is: 'self-pride ... stupidity, ferocious stupidity'.[21] Leavis does not appear to remember that Othello is an Elizabethan stage Moor.

Othello belongs to a second tradition which is often misunderstood — the tradition of the noble Moor. In its more general form, this tradition derives from classical literature. More immediately, it depends on the reports of several

Renaissance travellers, and on the exhaustive *Geographical Historie of Africa*. In the mythology of Greece and Rome, the Ethiopians — the 'sunburnt people' — were a morally blameless race living south of the Nile. According to Homer, their sacrificial feasts were attended by Poseidon, Iris, Menelaus and even Zeus. The country of these dark people lay in the path of the sun, hence their colour. In Greek art, these black people were treated according to one investigator with considerable charm because of their strange and novel physiognomy; and were quite idealised through the association with legendary Ethiopia.[22] In the literature, the Ethiopians remained a brave race whose king, the beautiful Memnon, son of the goddess Eos, fought bravely on the Trojan side during the Great War, killing the son of Nestor before being finally vanquished by Achilles. In Roman literature, Ethiopians were represented as a brave and daring race of men. Lucan, for example, describes a Numidian army made up of an assortment of peoples, 'Of the Negro hunter, whose habit is to stray through the deserted villages and smother lions in the folds of his garment, when he has lost confidence in his spear.'[23]

With the increase in the number of travellers to Africa, there was naturally an increase in the volume of descriptions about 'Ethiopia' and her peoples. There were stories of great princes and empires, of strange societies and customs. Apparently the most authoritative of these accounts was Leo Africanus' *Geographical Historie* (already referred to) which was translated into English in 1590 by John Pory. Leo, himself an African, was baptised and educated in Rome. His *Historie* was thus regarded as a first-hand account of the peoples and customs of the interior of Africa. In his book, Leo speaks of many royal Ethiopian families from which were descended noble princes such as Othello in fact claims to be: 'I fetch my life and being/From men of royal siege' (I. ii. 21–2). These 'noble' Moors, according to the account, were men 'delighted with all kind of civilities and modest behaviour'. Among them, 'it is accounted heinous for any man to utter in companie, any bawdie or unseemely worde'. About their women they were very particular, so that 'whomsoever they find but talking to their wives, they presently go about to murther him'. Their women will sometimes 'accept of a Kisse', Leo reports,

> but who so tempteth them farther, putteth his own life in hazard. For by reason of jealousie, you may see them daily, one to be the death and destruction of another, and that in such savage and brutish manner, that in any case they will shew no compassion at all. And they seeme to bee more wise in this behalfe then divers of our people for they will be no meanes match themselves unto an harlot.[24]

Because of this pride in their own nobility of nature, the royal Moor would not readily forgive personal affronts or insults but, '(according to the proverbe) they will deeply engrave in marble any injurie be it never so small and will in no wise blot it out of their remembrance.'[25]

We should expect, then, to see Othello as an embodiment of these racio-cultural characteristics of the noble Moor. Othello satisfies these expectations. Not only is he the noble Moor, he has the bravery of the very best of them. His account of his military exploits is in testimony of this. The Elizabethan audience would have been willing to suspend disbelief in these stories very much as Desdemona did; and they would have pitied him as well. Othello tells us that it was Brabantio, in fact, who requested to hear the story of his African life. 'I ran it through, even from my boyish days/To the very moment that he bade me tell it' (I. ii. 129–33). That Desdemona and her father believed Othello's tales of 'Cannibals, that each other eat;/The Anthropophagi, and men whose heads/Do grow beneath their shoulders' as *literally* true is no reason to suppose them more gullible than the rest of Venice, or than London. For Othello tells the same story to the Senators expecting them to believe it.[26] Othello's story must have been a typical Moor's story.

We may therefore say that Othello is an exo-cultural stereotype, meaning by that term, not that he is a 'flat' character, unmotivated and implausible, but that his characterisation is regulated by conditions assumed to be valid for the broad class of people called Moors. The plausibility of the characterisation is assured by the conditioning of the imagination of the audience to expect certain traits from a man with Othello's kind of background. That Othello is a Moor is not, consequently, a matter of detail: you cannot make Othello anything but a Moor and have the same play.

This argument can have its dangers. It could lead, for example, to the suggestion that Othello is suffering from an inferiority complex, to the effects of his failure to get assimilated. But the danger is a remote one, if the substance of my argument is fully appreciated. For it is part of my argument that Othello is not a real Moor, but a stage Moor, the creation of a particular culture for its own entertainment and instruction. In short, Othello is not 'a Moor', but 'Shakespeare's Moor'. And the unique fact about this Moor is that he is not merely a noble Moor, but a tragic Moor. Against the background of *Titus Andronicus* and the lustfulness of Aaron, Othello had to be chaste and modest; in contrast to Aaron's characterless Tamora, Othello's Desdemona had to be chaste and honourable. In any event, Othello had to redeem himself by appealing to those sentiments that would win him the sympathy of his audience. That is to say, Shakespeare had to make him do so. Othello could not have hated white Venice or insulted Desdemona's memory or boasted his Moorish character; an Othello who did would have become (like Marlowe's Barabas) a monster of an alien.

How does Shakespeare effect this manipulation of the Moor stereotype? Shakespeare lets us see Iago and Roderigo plan to abuse the mind of Desdemona's father by alleging an Aaron-like seduction which Othello promptly denies in his statement of clarification:

> That I have ta'en away this old man's daughter,
> It is most true: true; I have married her,
> The very head and front of my offending
> Hath this extent, no more.
>
> (I. iii. 78–81).

Then after the fury of the trial scenes, Shakespeare allows Brabantio to acquiesce in the 'marriage' and the Senate to concede that, contrary to all suspicions, Othello had not won Desdemona by devious means. Othello does not press any claims on Desdemona; he only defends his own good name. He does not resent the blunt remarks made by Brabantio in open court; he accepts them, even pledges to continue to devote himself to the service of the state. What begins his tragedy is not the marriage as such but the intervention of his Moorish psychology and the determination of Iago to have his revenge for alleged grievances. Without these two circumstances, Othello would have remained a complete noble soldier, reserved and controlled, a dutiful and obedient servant of Venice.

This picture of Othello gives us no hint of the possibility of extreme rage of which he soon shows himself capable. This is the important point. Till the temptation is over, Othello is the noble Moor, the 'perfect soul', the 'misbelieving Moor', as Marcus describes him in V. III. 121, 143. 'Who shall I swear by?' Lucius asks Aaron, 'thou believ'st no god'. Aaron answers: 'What if I do not? as, indeed, I do not' (V. i. 71, 73). Othello is different. 'For Christian shame,' he says, 'put by this barbarous brawl.' This is the Moor of Shakespeare's play; he does not become the terrible and doomed personality of the last scenes until the insinuation of Iago arouses a barbarism supposedly latent in him. Even so,

Shakespeare allows Othello to retain a certain kind of tragic dignity when, in spite of the frenzy he is in, he regains enough control of himself to see his strangling of Desdemona as an act of sacrifice rather than one of brutal sexual jealousy. In the bedchamber scene, the two traditions of the Moor merge: the potentialities of Othello the savage and the ideals of Othello the Christianised noble Moor are brought together and resolved in the 'radiant bliss' and the 'dreadful deformation' which Dover Wilson was grateful to see in Robeson's performance.

This scene has often been criticised, and wrongly too, it would seem. For it has not been always borne in mind that the murderer in the case is a Moor. What Shakespeare does in the scene needs to be carefully followed. First Shakespeare makes Desdemona an innocent and gentle creature, different from the typical faithless Venetian woman. In doing this, Shakespeare makes us believe that the Moor has been led (partly through his own gullibility) to suspect Desdemona of a thousand infidelities. 'I took you for that cunning whore of Venice, / That married with Othello' (V. ii. 91—2). Othello feels his honour tarnished by the scandal, and accordingly finds it impossible to endure. A noble Moor could not do worse than endure such scandal. Othello's prayer has made this clear:

> Had it pleas'd heaven
> To try me with affliction, had he rain'd
> All kinds of sores and shames on my bare head,
> Steep'd me in poverty, to the very lips,
> Given to captivity me and my hopes,
> I should have found in some part of my soul
> A drop of patience; . . . (VI. ii. 48—54)

The language is the language of Job and of the Old Testament. Othello had to speak some such language on an English stage. But the Old Testament motif is linked with a specifically Negro complaint — that of slavery. For as Othello himself tells us in I. iii. 138, he was rescued from slavery. His prayer here is thus a beautiful compounding of the trials of Job and that of the negro slave. Othello compares his blest condition — a free man, a soldier of fortune, a friend of the nobility — to the traditional alternative for the Moor — being sold into captivity. Othello is saying, therefore, that he would have preferred the condition of Job or of a Negro slave to his present predicament as a deceived husband. The exaggeration is perhaps strained, but it is not a joke: at least not if we recognise the plausibility of this indignation to the Elizabethan audience. For Othello's sense of personal affront at Desdemona's infidelity is supported by what was thought to be the noble (even if frightful) ethic of Othello's native Barbary.

But when Othello comes to the actual strangling of Desdemona, his fury takes a sudden ritual turn. Desdemona becomes the tragic victim of her own generosity of heart, as it were proving Cinthio's moralising right. Othello is now bent on the justice of his impending act; Cinthio's story seemed to insist on the inevitability of such a tragic conclusion. For Cinthio's story is not, as most editors like to suggest, merely a tale of a happy marriage broken by the intruding malice of the Moor's subordinates. Rather, it is an *exemplum* used to illustrate a thesis. That thesis, as Dover Wilson has put it, is that the 'secret of success in marriage . . . must be looked for in spiritual union of the partners, though (Cinthio) suggests that this kind of union is difficult to maintain if husband and wife, owing to the circumstances of their birth or upbringing, have a different outlook on life, or have been accustomed to different modes of living.' The story of Cinthio's Desdemona thus illustrates a possible fatal conclusion to an ill-matched marriage. Desdemona herself declares that her fate is a warning to Italian girls not to marry a man divided from them by race (*la Natura*), religion (*il Cielo*) and manner of life (*il modo della vita*).[27] In Shakespeare's play, Gratiano says as much; or, more precisely, he makes a speech which can be understood in no other way than that he assumes as much:

> Poor Desdemona, I am glad thy father's dead;
> Thy match was mortal to him, and pure grief
> Shore his old thread atwain: did he live now,
> This sight would make him do a desperate turn, . . .
> And fall to reprobation. (V. ii. 205–10)

In Othello's famous soliloquy, V. ii. 1–22, 'It is the cause', Shakespeare unobtrusively but unmistakeably underpins this view of the situation. Othello's speech keeps before the audience not just Desdemona's beauty, but her white and innocent beauty — by implication, the white and innocent beauty that she has so generously and tragically entrusted to this black, noble but different man. There is still no question of interpreting Othello as suffering from the isolation of an alien — Desdemona is not his hostage in a white Venice. But she is associated (through tragically ironic contrast) with 'the balmy breath' that 'doth almost persuade/Justice herself to break her sword'; above all, her skin is 'that whiter skin of hers than snow'. Othello is thus made to pay what is indirectly a tribute to an ideal of white womanhood that he has earlier held and, as he thinks, found false. The effect of the worship is to establish the tragic — tragic especially because inherent — gap between Othello's inalienable sense of Moorish justice and the true character of the act he is about to perform. He could not have done otherwise than he is about to do: his murder of Desdemona can be reconciled to his worship of her on no other grounds than this. His act follows from his Moorish character, and Shakespeare presents him as torn between his worship of the white goddess and the carrying out of a necessary barbaric cleansing.

Shakespeare devotes much time to Othello's state of mind in this last scene, and Othello's many speeches have accordingly become the subject of much critical comment and controversy. T. S. Eliot, for example, in a famous comment, says of the last speech that the Moor is merely

> cheering himself up. He is endeavouring to escape reality, he has ceased to think about Desdemona, and is thinking about himself . . . Othello succeeds in turning himself into a pathetic figure, by adopting an *aesthetic* rather than a moral attitude, dramatising himself against his environment. He takes in the spectator, but the human motive is primarily to take in himself.[28]

F. R. Leavis develops this argument, and calls Othello's speech 'self-dramatisation as unself-comprehending as before'. 'Contemplating the spectacle of himself, Othello is overcome with the pathos of it.'[29] More recently Barbara Everett has accused Leavis both of 'a hatred and fear of the "heroic", the large, the universal, the self-sufficient, the grandiose, the rhetorical,' and of 'using the words ('action' and 'acting') to carry (an) implicit . . . condemnation.' Like Eliot, she sees Othello's speech in V. ii. 343—52

> . . . of one whose hand
> Like the base Indian, threw a pearl away,
> Richer than all his tribe; of one whose subdued eyes,
> Albeit unused to the melting mood,
> Drop tears as fast as the Arabian trees
> Their medicinal gum; . . .

as crucial. 'Othello is mourning for himself — but himself as representative of a whole destroyed world: he is 'heroic' in the sense in which Donne is heroic . . . The impersonalised lyrical and rhetorical images . . . take the situation beyond Othello to a world at once barbaric and Christian, *universal in its range*' (my italics).[30]

It is more likely, in fact, that Shakespeare is coping with a situation theatrically more concrete than these critics have noticed. I have spoken earlier of the danger of the kind of 'character criticism' which would attribute to Othello during the action of the play a neurotic sense of being a black alien in a white world. At the same time I have argued that Othello's behaviour in the play remains within the limits imposed by — even underwrites — two of the stereotype conceptions of a Moor likely to be held by Shakespeare's audience. We are now at a point of the play where it is no longer necessary to distinguish between the two stereotypes governing Othello's action; but he is — above all in the theatre — still a Moor.

> And say besides, that in Aleppo once,
> Where a malignant and a turban'd Turk
> Beat a Venetian and traduc'd the state,
> I took by the throat the circumcised dog,
> And smote him thus. (V. ii. 355–9)

Having once, as a 'noble Moor', passed judgment on his supposedly adulterous wife, Othello is now once more, as the servant of the Venetian state, passing judgement on the barbarous Othello who killed 'a Venetian' — the Othello who has behaved as an infidel or outsider, a 'Turk'. And I suggest that he passes judgement so in view of a peculiar theatrical necessity. Shakespeare has here a double problem. For if by a concluding tragic action he has finally to establish Othello's personal identity, both individual, and, as Barbara Everett says, universal (the full dramatic illusion of life of an autonomous human being with reason and free will), he has also to win back for Othello his audience's sympathy which Othello by his action has, in the full sense of the word, alienated. *At this point in the play, clearly, the sympathy of the Elizabethan audience in the theatre will to a large extent coincide with that of Othello's Venetian audience within the play.* The fact, then, is that in his last speech Othello is

apologising to both audiences for the murder of Desdemona
in the only way it is possible for him to do so. For when all is
said, he is not as important to Venice as Desdemona is. His
death will be a loss to the military plans of Venice ('I have
done the state some service, and they know't') but it is
primarily an alien's death, the death 'of one whose hand/Like
the base Indian, threw a pearl away/Richer than all his tribe.'
Sad as it is, it will not provoke in an Elizabethan audience
that particular sense of loss that the death of a loved public
figure (Hamlet or Lear) who belongs to a community excites
in the members of that community and in the audience.

Othello is thus under a peculiar necessity to play a double
role; it is part of his private tragedy that he must be
peculiarly aware of his public image. He seems, indeed, —
though not for the reasons Eliot and Leavis suggest — to need
an audience; and left alone with Desdemona's body, after
Emilia's death, his first action is for no apparent reason to
call in Gratiano to listen to him reflect on his fall and folly.

> Here is my journey's end, here is my butt,
> And very sea-mark of my utmost sail.
> > *. . . Where should Othello go?*
> > (V. ii. 265—9, 272; my italics)

By torturing himself in Gratiano's presence for this folly,
Othello is saving himself from an inevitable public obloquy.
Eliot's and Leavis's arguments about that speech, and Miss
Everett's too, thus all miss the point. Othello may be
'self-dramatising', but he is not '*contemplating* the spectacle
of himself', nor is he himself 'overcome with the pathos of
it' — he is a black alien *offering* the spectacle of himself for
his white audience to be moved by the pathos of it:

> Whip me, you devils,
> From the possession of this heavenly sight,
> Blow me about in winds, roast me in sulphur,

Wash me in steep-down gulfs of liquid fire!
O Desdemona, Desdemona dead,
Oh, oh, oh. (V. ii. 278—83)

Having thus effected (in public) a private reconciliation with
his God, Othello turns to face the Venetian public to explain
his conduct, in the speech I have already discussed.

Lodovico seems to have believed in Othello's inherent
weakness. He does not accuse him of murder, as he might
have done. He only calls him 'this rash and most unfortunate
man' (V. ii. 284). Lodovico then divests him of his command
to invest in Cassio. When Othello commits suicide, Lodovico
simply bequeathes the Moor's possessions on Gratiano:

> . . . Gratiano, keep the house,
> And seize upon the fortunes of the Moor,
> For they succeed to you: . . . (V. ii. 366—8)

Othello's speech of self-explanation is in fact almost his only
eulogy. He was after all connected with Venice in a mercen-
ary arrangement. Having fouled his career by the murder of
Desdemona, suicide was the only redeeming act possible to
him. The greatest tribute paid to him is Lodovico's amazement.

> O thou Othello, that wert once so good,
> Fall'n in the practice of a damned slave,
> What should be said to thee? (V. ii. 292—4)

After the suicide, there is only Cassio's brief comment: 'This
did I fear, but thought he had no weapon,/For he was great
of heart' (V. ii. 361—2) No other Shakespearean hero suffers
as purposeless a tragedy as Othello; none other is eulogised as
he is in an after-thought.

It remains to relate this discussion to the tradition of a
Christian and symbolic reading of *Othello*, especially to the

usual equation of Othello with the devil. While the tradition of the savage and the noble Moor give plausibility to Othello's behaviour, the Christian tradition gives a unique importance to his significance and virtually makes a symbol of him. Our intention in this part of the chapter is to examine the implications of this identification for the play and for the criticism of the character of its hero.

ꭗ When Othello calls Iago 'that demi-devil' in a reply to a question from Cassio; when, too, Lodovico adds that Iago is 'the hellish villain' (V. ii. 302, 369), we know that they are speaking metaphorically. We assume that the description derives from an evaluation by the two speakers of the role of Iago in the play. We are in a position to regard the equation of Iago with the devil as a dramatic statement, as part of Shakespeare's deliberate effort to underline some of the symbolic meanings of Iago's character.

But when Emilia replies to Othello's charge that Desdemona is 'like a liar gone to burning hell', by calling Othello 'the blacker devil', 'thou art a devil' (V. ii. 130, 132, 134), we cannot so simply take her words as intended by Shakespeare to make us regard Othello as a mere devil symbol and Desdemona as angel. He may have intended less than this, or more. This is so because Othello is also called 'devil' even when there is no suggestion that he is like one; because the equation of black with the devil and the Negro had become a habit of speech in European literature which no longer reflected the serious disposition of either speaker or dramatist.

There was, indeed, a serious tradition of the black-with-devil equation in Elizabethan literature. Aaron is referred to as a 'hellish dog' in *Titus Andronicus*, IV. ii. 78. Lucius calls him 'the devil' in the very next Act: 'Bring down the devil for he must not die/So sweet a death as hanging presently' — to which Aaron replies: 'If there be devils, would I were a devil/To live and burn in everlasting fire' (V. i. 145–6; 147–9). Aaron's son by Tamora is also associated with the devil. Demetrius calls the child 'the offspring of so foul a fiend' (IV. ii. 79). The Nurse describes him as 'that which I would hide from heaven's eye/Our empress' shame.'

> *Aar*   What hath he sent her?
> *Nurse*   A devil.
> *Aar*   Why, then she's the devil's dam: a joyful issue.
> *Nurse*   A joyless, dismal, black and sorrowful issue.
>
> (IV. ii. 59—60, 64—7)

Later in the play, speaking to the Goth, Lucius refers to Aaron as 'the incarnate devil' and to Aaron's son by Tamora as 'this growing image of thy fiend-like face' (V. i. 40—45). And even Eleazer of *Lust's Dominion* who explains that his heart is as white as snow, is nevertheless called 'a Moor, a devil, a slave of barbary, a dog.'[31]

These two aspects of the devil parallels — the seriously pejorative and the merely neutral — affect the reading of *Othello* and should be properly understood. Through association with darkness and night, blackness has been used in European literature as a sign of evil, even in pre-Christian times. Solon speaks of the 'black heart' meaning an unresponsive heart. Diphilus speaks of woman as a 'black' character. Plutarch advises a young man not to spend his time with a black man, that is, a man of ill repute. Lucian tells us of a house-haunting demon who was squalid, black-haired and 'darker than gloom'.[32] These uses were, however, metaphorical. Apart from Juvenal's fifth satire which claims that a Negro is a sign of ill luck — 'cui per mediam molis occurrere noctem' — there is surprisingly no automatic identification of the Negro with evil in Latin and Greek literature. The individual character could be 'black' (or 'white'), but not the race.

In the literature of the Christian era, however, the Negro is called the 'devil' with a regularity and a matter-of-factness which would suggest that it must at some time have been regarded as a literal truth. In the post-medieval era, with increased loss of faith in over-simplified clerical categories, it became increasingly difficult to tell, in any given instance, whether the use of the blackness-devil equivalence is meant to be a statement of fact or a manner of speaking. For example, Zanthia in *The Knight of Malta*, is called 'hell's perfect character', a 'night hag of her black sire, the devil.' 'Hell cannot parch her blacker than she is.'[33] If we are tempted not to believe that a literal meaning was intended in this case, we should also remember that these descriptions had parallels in popular travel literature which were not meant to be read symbolically. An example is Caxton's attempt to establish the etymology for the names of the continents. Asia, he wrote, 'taketh the name of a quene that somtyme was lady of this regyon and was clled Asia'. Europe 'taketh his name of a kynge called Europes the which was lord of this contre; & therefore it was so called.' Africa, however, 'hath his name of helle.'[34] About the devil being 'sire' to Zanthia we have the evidence of Friar Joanno dos Santos who published his *Voyage and Historie* in 1597. In it, he reports seeing 'some Parents as black as Pitch, have white Goldi-locked children like Flemmings' — presumably albinos. These children, he says, were 'the Children of the Devil, begotten of blacke women by him when they are asleepe'[35] — an explanation which recalls Shakespeare's story in *The Tempest*. There is here a combination of fact and fancy exactly as we have it in the drama. A Negro character who is described as the devil thus lives in two worlds. The symbolic function he serves in the play is supported by the literal truth of his devilishness. If he is actually devilish in character, then he is only confirming a native satanism. If, like Othello, he is not evil, then he is a redeemed devil likely to fall back into hell if he does not save himself through conversion from the inner compulsions of his nature.

To return to *Othello*. While Iago is a 'devil' as a matter of personal guilt, Othello is one as a matter of fact. Brabantio's comment, 'Damned as thou art, thou hast enchanted her', was more than an insult: it was a statement of a kind of 'fact'. For Othello is damned, according to European tradition, in two simple senses. He shared the curse by which Lucifer was turned from the beautiful angel of light to the sooty prince of hell. He also inherited the curse placed by Noah on the children of Cham because of their father's irreverence, his lustfulness and his dishonesty.[36] In either sense he was a 'damned' man. But because he is a good man, a baptised man, he is freed from the curse for as long as he can sustain the Christian temperance which the new religion imposed on him. When he fails himself through the temptation of Iago, his plight quite naturally becomes even more pitiable and more pathetic to the Christian imagination. And Othello made very much of his Christianity. He labours to prepare Desdemona for the next life: 'I would not kill thy unprepared spirit,/No, heaven forfend, I would not kill thy soul' (V. ii. 31—2). Iago tells us that Desdemona could win the Moor to do anything, even if it should be his greatest treasure — 'to renounce his baptism/All seals and symbols of redeemed sin.' At the very end Othello himself realises that his murder of Desdemona will lead him to hell:

> when we shall meet at count,
> This look of thine will hurl my soul from heaven,
> And fiends will snatch at it: . . . (V. ii. 276—8)

One aspect of Othello's tragedy is this relapse into damnation; his nobility, from the Elizabethan point of view, lies in his recognition of the fact of this damnation. This recognition, surely, is an experience unique to the Moorish convert, and it is therefore redundant to speak of his damnation as one would that of a European Christian. For the pathos of Othello's final predicament is directly related to the fact of his exo-cultural status. The recognition which he shows of the value of his Christian conversion more than compensates for his inevitable (and unfortunate) betrayal of his Christian virtue! The damnation of Othello, whatever that is, serves to win him the sympathy of his audience. It is thus a most tragic (because an unintended) damnation.

That is why the elaborate symbolism detailed by S. L. Bethell and Paul N. Siegel about the Christian interpretation of Othello's perdition seems so extravagant. Both argue that by killing Desdemona, Othello commits a sin against the Holy Ghost — the unforgivable sin, and so goes to Hell. According to Siegel, Othello brings 'chaos to his moral being and perdition to his soul, having traduced divine goodness and violated the law of God.'[3][7] The limitations to this argument have been pointed out sufficiently by other critics. What needs stressing here is that the matter of Othello's salvation is finally less relevant than Bethel and Siegel suggest to the criticism of a character who does not *belong* to the world of the audience. It is enough for the audience in Othello's case that he should give sufficient public indication of his awareness of his error, and of his repentance. Othello does this beautifully by subordinating his own downfall in concern for Desdemona's soul being saved. Rymer was right, in a sense, in noting that Othello doted on Desdemona's soul 'as (he) had been her *Father Confessor*.'[3][8] Othello, the Elizabethan stage Moor, could have shown no greater proof of greatness, or of heroic maturity than this. His tragic greatness was, after all, *sui generis*.

4 The Exo-cultural Hero of the Enlightenment

This chapter is really a footnote to the history of the idea of the 'savage hero' of the Enlightenment. It seeks to qualify some of the critical conclusions usually reached about the status of the 'savage' stereotype in the literature of that period. It argues that the period, unlike the Elizabethan age, failed to achieve an effective literary representation of the 'savage hero' because it was unable to accept the consequences of its own deep-seated imaginative attitudes.

Lovejoy's essays on Rousseau and Monboddo have, indeed, corrected some of the oversimplifications of earlier historians of the idea of primitivism.[1] Yet, the implications of his reinterpretation of Rousseau's *Second Discourse* have not been fully applied to the criticism of the literature of the period. If it is true, as Lovejoy argues, that the philosophers of the Enlightenment were not uninhibited worshippers of the savage man, it would imply that the so-called 'distinctively revolutionary relativism in political and social philosophy'[2] which these philosophers advocated was bound to have its own kind of expression in imaginative literature. An almost perversely introspective age, the Enlightenment looked up to the voyagers and the biologists for evidence that would help resolve their philosophical concerns and perplexities. Lacking a single coherent (and almost theological) explanation for the seemingly infinite variety of human society as the Elizabethans had, the imaginative writers of the period adopted an arbitrary but convenient attitude to what they saw as the problem-child of mankind — the so-called Indian and Negro savage; a problem-child, because the schema and the predispositions of the eighteenth-century led them on some occasions to consider the savage as an outright orang outang and at other times to see him as an angel. What resulted from their questionings was hardly a humanistic and heartfelt celebration of the savage hero (as Fairchild, Sypher and others imply)[3] but, in fact, an equivocal and possibly an arrogant attempt at the domestication of a mystery. There is no greater measure of their difference from the Elizabethan period than this.

From this point of view *the* true savage of the Shakespearen corpus is Caliban rather than Aaron or Othello. Caliban retains all the pejorative qualities associated with this type and in his half-real, half-fictional world conjures up a most telling impression of the nature and the implications of the savage mentality. He is the exo-cultural hero in the most absolute sense. It is easy enough to see that Caliban is meant to serve a powerful symbolic function in *The Tempest*; and it would not matter much whether we see this function in terms of Christian concepts of ethical and political morality, of neoplatonic doctrines, or of Renaissance ideas about white and black magic. James E. Phillips says,

> All agree that in Caliban, Shakespeare intended to represent some form of life or activity below that of civilized man, whether it be the primitive savage encountered in England's colonial ventures, the monster frequently described in contemporary travel literature, the devil-daemon of black magic and medieval Christian tradition, or the cannibal from which his name seems to be derived.[5]

Certainly the demonstrably contradictory elements of his character strongly suggest such a symbolic importance. On the one hand, he has a passionate, though perverse, love of music, a strong but also perverted sense of the Godhead and an earnest almost revolutionary desire for freedom. On the other hand, he is represented as incapable of appreciating 'the good', of self-restraint and of judgement (or reason). Hence, though he is treated quite cruelly by Prospero, Caliban is nevertheless seen as undeserving of freedom and independence in a fundamental sense. He is, thus, as far outside the culture of the Elizabethan audience (as well, too, of Prospero's society) as can be. In this sense, Caliban is a *slave* because, in absolute terms, he is incapable of deriving any benefit from education or social intercourse and cannot therefore live in civil society. Prospero taught him language, but his 'profit on't/Is I know how to curse. The red plague rid you/For learning me your language (I. ii. 363—5). Because he lacks all moral sense, he repays Miranda's 'kindness' by attempting to violate her chastity. As Phillips has argued, Caliban may well represent what the Renaissance called the 'vegetative' part of the Soul, the housekeeper and slave of the two higher parts — the 'Rational' and the 'Sensitive'. 'Suffice it to say that the Renaissance moral philosophers repeatedly insisted that, in so far as man as concerned, the vegetative soul is simply the servant of the higher human powers', represented principally by Ariel and Prospero.[6]

But though Caliban can be seen as representing the fallen man or the brute in man, yet it is clear that he also derives much of his being from contemporary notions of the savage, that there was a predisposition on the part of the Elizabethan audience to equate the cannibal (Caliban) with the devil and the brute with 'vegetative soul' in a simple and unabashed manner. It is this predisposition, in fact, that makes his symbolic meanings both straightforward and powerful. As John E. Hankins put it, Caliban is represented as the child of an African witch from Algeria, though he is said to worship a Patagonian god.[7] In this sense, Caliban is one limit to the possibilities of dramatising the brutish man or the savage. In him all the qualities and characteristics of the type are combined and given dramatic authenticity. That he has become in our time a symbol of the expropriated colonial man is nothing against this fact.

Trinculo was reluctant to call Caliban a man. 'Were I in England now,' he says, 'as once I was, and had but this fish painted, not a holiday fool there but would give a piece of silver; there would this monster make a man; any strange beast there makes a man; when they will not give a doit to relieve a lame beggar, they will lay out ten to see a dead Indian' (II. ii. 29—34). Though he claims it here, Trinculo is not really less credulous than the contemporary Englishman. Sir Walter Raleigh himself, in his *Historie of the World* (1614), was equally puzzled as to the status of the various peoples whom the explorers were discovering in Africa and the Indies. 'If colour or magnitude made a difference of *species*, then were the Negroes which we call *Black-Mores, non animalia rationalia*, not men, but some kind of strange Beasts: and so the Giants of the South *America* should be of another kind, then the people of this part of the world.'[8] The crucial contrast is, of course, between *animalia rationalia* and 'strange beasts', between men and cannibal monsters (such as Caliban), blackamoors and giants of South America. Between them, choice was not always easy. In that contrast, accordingly, lay the enlightened credulity of the Elizabethans which produced Othello and enabled Caliban to live in a world partly of reality and partly of fiction. His existence was propped up by a climate of opinion which was already conditioned to entertain the possibility (admittedly an extravagant but theologically defensible one) that there were such man-beasts as Shakespeare had created in *The Tempest*.[9]

The Enlightenment lacked the courage to sustain a similar predisposition, and this lack is, ultimately, responsible for the absurdity of the representation of the savage hero — whether African or Indian — in the literature of the period. The Elizabethans maintained a fairly coherent and consistent attitude to these peoples, as savages and as noble men. The literature of the period reflected this attitude with integrity, frankness and power. The writers of the Enlightenment, on the other hand, tried to affect a polite and rationalised attitude to the African and the Indian in disregard of those deep-rooted feelings about them which had become part of the tradition of Christian Europe. Inspite of its conscious effort to effect a *literary* transformation of the savage into a heroic and holy figure, the Enlightenment was nevertheless unwilling to accept the physical and moral features of its new-found hero. The consequence is a divided conscience which was prepared to celebrate the savage hero as the untutored sage and saint of the jungle, but was unprepared to change those attitudes of mind which stood in the way of a truly valid representation of such a character. The so-called Age of Reason was, in this connection, an Age of Absurdity.

It has become traditional in histories of literature to explain away this ambiguity of attitude by citing the influence of Montaigne and the primitivists who brought a long tradition of the (European) noble savage cult to its final stage. In the words of H. N. Fairchild, 'by fusing the more or less objective and irreflective narrations of the explorers with various long-current traditions, the philosopher arrives at important generalizations about the virtue of savage man and the deteriorating effects of civilization.'[10] This is true. The accounts of travellers and the musings of philosophers led to the development of this cult. But what really sustained it was not so much the so-called savage himself as the disillusionment of Europe over its civilisation and its values. The tropical Utopia of the Elizabethans was only indirectly contrasted with the actual world of Christian Europe and their paradise was invariably a fictional (or, at heart, a mythical) recreation of the biblical and the classical prototypes. The utopia of the Enlightenment was created in a direct attempt to highlight the paradox of a civilised but imperfect Europe. The aspirations of the one age were represented by the *Utopia* and *New Atlantis*, the anxieties and frustrations of the other by *Robinson Crusoe, Gulliver's Travels* and *Rasselas, Prince of Abyssinia*.

Primitivism in this sense was a kind of therapy to Europe's spiritual ills. 'Any imperious want in the mentality of an age,' Preserved Smith has said, 'will call forth the fabrication of ideas to supply it.'[11] The so-called cult of the noble savage was such a fabrication. It was a reaction against the urban civilisation of Europe and an indirect plea for the cultivation of the simple virtues which, by contrast, it sought to associate with the 'primitive' and 'pastoral' world of the non-European peoples. It was the product of Reason reacting against itself in the tradition of Erasmian anti-scholasticism. School-knowledge, Erasmus had argued in *The Praise of Folly*, was the creation of the devil, and was unknown to the simple people of the Golden Age for whom 'nature' was sufficient. Logic was unnecessary to men among whom no arguments arose. Block-heads were the happiest of people for they were not only devoid of the dread of death, they had no accusing consciences to make them fear it. They felt no shame, no solicitude, no ambition, no envy and no love. The Enlightenment pushed this anti-scholasticist philosophy to an ultimate conclusion by asserting that the 'unlearned' savage was by nature better than the man of reason who had been 'bastardized' through 'the pleasure of our corrupted taste'.[12]

This argument had originally nothing to do with the savage, since the essential contrast was between the school-man and the illiterate peasant, between the urban man and the rustic. Moreover, these contrasts were established *within* the culture of Europe. But the logic of the argument demanded its extension to the Indian and the African, not because of a prior belief in the fact, but because such an extension represented a kind of healthy *reductio ad absurdum*. If the Erasmian contention was right, so the argument ran, then the Indian who was said to be mentally inferior to children and fools must be by far superior to the civilised man of Europe. His actual inferiority was, in fact, a condition for this supposed superiority.

The cult of primitivism was, therefore, first and last, an

intellectual exercise. Its effect was to modify the patterns of thought rather than of feeling, to humour rather than excite the imagination. Primitivism was Europe's way of asserting its new mood of optimism in human nature. As the Cambridge Platonist, Nathaniel Culverwell put it:

> Look upon the diversities of Nations and there you will see a rough and barbarous Scythian, a wild American, an unpolish'd Indian, a superstitious Aegyptian, a subtle Ethiopian, a cunning Arabian, a luxurious Persian . . . and many other heaps of Nations, . . . and tell me whether it must not be some admirable and efficacious Truth, that shall so overpower them all, as to pass current amongst them, and be owned and acknowledged by them.[13]

In this sense, Rousseau's *Second Discourse* was an attempt to return to commonsense after the fanciful theorisings of the enthusiasts. In it, it becomes very clear that the concern with savages was originally intended to illustrate a contention of immediate relevance to the civilisation of Europe. Rousseau plots a scale of 'conditions' or 'states' between beasts and rational men and argues that the savage 'commencera par les fonctions purement animales. Apercevoir et sentir sera son premier etat, qui lui sera commun avec tous les animaux.' Primitive life shows us creatures characterised by the worst degree of '*pesanter et stupidite*' and destitute of moral ideas of any kind.[14]

Properly understood, then, the cult of the noble savage in the period of the Enlightenment was really a failed effort at the baptism of the savage, a futile attempt to erase the conditioning of centuries from the imagination of Europe. It is, therefore, important to assert that the effort failed, and to know how and why.

Defoe's *Robinson Crusoe* is usually held up as an example of the glorification of the savage in the literature of the Enlightenment. Defoe's Man Friday is regarded as one of the products of this incorrigible tendency to idealise the Indian savage. One basis for this attitude is Defoe's description of him as 'a comely, handsome fellow, perfectly well-made, with straight strong limbs, not too large; tall, well-shaped, and as I reckon, about twenty-six years of age.'[15] This description would, at first sight, appear to be proof of Defoe's acceptance of the noble savage tradition, as an indication of his readiness to accept the possibility of a handsome perfectly well-made Indian. The fact is, however, that though Defoe is obviously anxious to show his Indian to be comely, he is equally at pains to show that he is an exception to a more general rule. His general description of Man Friday is accordingly surrounded with qualifications and modifications which have the effect of making Friday more European than Indian. As far as the conditioned imagination of the age was concerned, Man Friday had to be un-Indian to be beautiful, as these passages attest. 'He had a very good countenance, not a fierce and surly aspect; but seemed to have something very manly in his face; and yet he had all the sweetness and softness of an European in his countenance too, especially when as he smiled.' Beyond this description of the Indian in terms of a European norm, Defoe proceeds to distinguish Man Friday from what must be regarded as typical Indian or negroid man:

> His hair was long and black, not curled like wool; his forehead very high and large; and a great vivacity and sparkling sharpness in his eyes. The colour of his skin was not quite black, but very tawny; . . . His face was round and plump; his nose small, not flat like the Negroes; a very good mouth, thin lips and his fine teeth well set, and white as ivory (p. 199).

Not only is he unlike the Negro in these important respects, Man Friday is equally unlike his fellow Indians. Defoe describes him as 'tawny', but he is not 'of an ugly, yellow, nauseous tawny, as the Brazilians and Virginians, and other natives of America are; but a bright kind of a dun olive colour that had in it something very agreeable, though not very easy to describe.' Professor Fairchild has correctly remarked that the 'care taken by Defoe to distinguish Friday's appearance from that of Negroes and less attractive Indian tribes is worthy of notice... Defoe was evidently afraid that Friday, unless carefully described, would suggest to the reader's mind a negroid type.'[16] One should add that Defoe has merely created an Indian which his feelings and the imagination of his civilisation could *accept* as beautiful. A character with woolly hair, flat nose and thick lips would have been unacceptable to that imagination as beautiful and Defoe would have thought it preposterous to describe such a character as 'comely and handsome'. It is not, moreover, as if Defoe were trying to establish some factual accuracy in his description of Man Friday. For not only is Man Friday of a shade of 'tawny' so subtle as to be 'not very easy to describe', he is unlike *any other* of his tribesmen. Defoe's beautiful Indian turns out, in actual fact, to be a local miracle.

A similar confusion appears in Mrs Aphra Behn's *Oroonoko, or The Royal Slave.* There we find that though the hero is said to be an African, he is un-African in every important respect. His native country, Coromantien, is said to be 'a Country of *Blacks* so-called'.[17] He is said to be 'adorned with a native Beauty, so transcending all those of his gloomy Race, that he struck an Awe and Reverence, even into those that knew not his quality' (p. 134). The description ought, indeed, to be quoted at length.

His face was not of that brown rusty black which most of that nation are, but of a perfect Ebony, or polished jet. His eyes were the most aweful that could be seen and very piercing; the white of 'em being like snow, as were his Teeth. His Nose was rising and *Roman*, instead of African and flat. It's Mouth the finest shaped that could be seen;

far from those great turn'd lips, which one so natural to the rest of the Negroes. The whole Proportion, and Air of his Face was so nobly and exactly form'd, that *bating his colour* (italics added), there could be nothing in Nature more beautiful, agreeable and handsome (p. 136).

The handsome man of Mrs Behn's imagination was not African at all, in spite of his 'perfect Ebony' or 'polished Jet' colour. Oroonoko is not, therefore, so much an example of a willingness to believe in the noble Negro as an illustration of the irresolution which the Enlightenment foisted on itself by attempting to circumvent the realities of its deep-seated attitudes and predispositions.

Not only is the black hero of this period shown to be different in his features from other black men, he is shown to be an isolated example of virtue or nobility among his people. Whereas the hero is presented as loyal slave or as the morally upright hero, all his fellow countrymen are presented as truly dangerous and unpleasantly barbarous. One soon realises that the heroism or the uprightness being celebrated in an individual character is not a quality generally associated with, usually manifested in his race, but some isolated manifestation. Defoe's 'noble' Friday is said to be loyal and friendly, he nevertheless belongs to a 'most brutish and barbarous race of savages.' Crusoe 'entertained such an abhorrence of the savage wretches . . . and of their wretched, inhuman custom of their devouring and eating one another up, that I continued pensive and sad, and kept close within my own circle for almost two years after this . . . for the aversion which Nature gave me to these hellish wretches was such that I was fearful of seeing them as of seeing the Devil himself.'[18] Friday's moral 'beauty' must have been a miraculous surprise to Crusoe.

Similarly, Oroonoko is a lone gem among his brutish people. His grandfather is a wicked and promiscuous man. His slaves condone his excesses and even help him to compromise the virtue of Imoinda. We hear of Oroonoko's heroic exploits before his capture, but these exploits are carried out against a background of barbarous, even cruel, life which is of interest simply because of its operatic and macabre quality. Otherwise, Oroonoko is a typical prince of England. He boasts of his personal accomplishment in the manners of a typical European prince of his period; he parades his knowledge of French and Spanish and his up to date information on the fortunes of the English Civil War. In Southern's version of the story, Oroonoko displays his difference from the other slaves and from the Indians of the island by leading an offensive that rescues Imoinda. The Governor says to him:

> Thou glorious man! thou something greater sure
> Than Caesar ever was! that single arm
> Has sav'd us all: accept our general thanks.[19]

In George Coleman's *Inkle and Yarico*, the black heroine, Yarico, herself has a negro slave. She speaks of her brothers as savages and warns her white friends: 'and do you know the danger that surrounds you? Our woods are filled with beasts of prey — my countrymen too ... might kill you.' At one point in the play, we have a series of episodes in which some of the Europeans are shown 'pursued by Blacks'. The heroine is thus as much unlike her brothers as can be. What Coleman is praising is, thus, the exception rather than the norm; Yarico had to be 'baptised' clean of her *essentially* Indian or African ancestry and converted into a possible English woman in a tropical setting.

Quite as important is this inability of the Enlightenment to accept a genuinely black man as a hero is the fact that the representation of the Negro as a loyal slave stereotype succeeds more often than that of the noble Negro. That is to say, the loyal-negro type appears to the European mind to be a more plausible character, *in any context*, than his royal counterpart. This is of particular significance because many of the authors who wrote plays or novels about the African were seriously involved in the Abolition Movement. It is strange, therefore, that they should themselves regard the slave condition as *natural* to the Negro. Though they speak against cruel slave owners in their work, these writers do not challenge the assumption (on which the slave-stereotype was based) that the Negro was ordained to serve. Southern's attempts in his *Oroonoko* to represent the nature of white cruelty towards the Negro slave leave the reader with the feeling that despite his strenuous efforts, he is really incapable of representing this cruelty successfully. When the planters, for example, hear of Oroonoko and the manner in which he was captured, they indeed express their gratitude to the treacherous captain:

> *2nd Planter* Such men as you [the Captain] are fit to be employed in public affairs: the plantation will thrive by you.
>
> *3rd Planter* Industry ought to be encouraged.
>
> *Captain* There's nothing done without it, boys. I have made my fortune this way.

It is true that Southern introduces two Englishmen, Blandford and Stanmore, to condemn the callousness of these planters,[20] but their protest does not question the principle of slavery; it only serves as a reminder to the English audience of the shortcomings of their countrymen abroad. The resentment expressed by Stanmore and Blandford is not a passionate condemnation of slavery but an elegant disapproval of unmannerly conduct, and is part of a ritual directed at a civilised but faulted Europe. Both men are saying, in effect, that these planters are not reputable enough representatives of European civilisation and Christian morality.

The inability of these writers to represent genuine anti-slavery sentiment is a negative aspect of their use of the negro slave stereotype. The positive aspect is their tacit acceptance of the *natural loyalty* of the Negro servant. This loyalty is regarded almost as a racial trait, and is seen as so unique that it is never compared to the personal loyalty of the European servant to his master. The form which the feeling about the Negro takes in the writers of the eighteenth century is interesting. Though Mrs Aphra Behn's novel is directed against the enslavement of its hero, we are told that this hero was at one time a slave-dealer. When he is himself captured and sold to America, he is said to have been welcomed very warmly by the slaves, some of whom recognised him as their captor in Africa. At the slave camp, these slaves

> . . . all come forth to behold him, and found he was that Prince who had, at several times, sold most o'em to these Parts; and from a Veneration they pay to great Men, especially if they know 'em, and from the surprize and Awe they had at the sight of him, they all cast themselves at his Feet, crying out, in their language, *Live O King! Long Live, O King!* and kissing his Feet, paid him even Divine Homage.[21]

Since the intention in *Oroonoko* was to arouse popular feeling against slavery, it is surprising that the slaves do not show any sign of discontent. It is more surprising that when, indeed, the slaves attempt a revolt from their cruel masters, both Mrs Aphra Behn and Southern condemn their action. It would appear, then, that these writers found nothing intrinsically wrong in the enslavement of the Negro if only he was well treated, that they were objecting not to the enslavement of a Negro but to that of a noble prince, and that they disapproved of the attempt to disturb the *status quo* by liberating the common slave of the plantations.

In *Robinson Crusoe* we have the perfect example of the slave stereotype. The situation that develops between Crusoe and Friday is particularly interesting since it has been generally regarded by commentators as an instance of a genuine fraternal relationship developing between master and slave. Fairchild claims that 'the sympathy and understanding that spring up between the two represent on a small scale the feelings which would bind all men together if they turned inward to their hearts instead of outward to the world.'[2 2] According to Wylie Sypher, Defoe succeeds in making the savage a fellow-being. 'Not until the end of the century is there a realism comparable to his, even though the facts were more readily available to later novelists. His impassioned analysis is also wanting in later fiction. Few novelists deal with slavery so competently.'[2 3] In fact, however, the difficulty is in Sypher's not recognising Friday's status as an exo-cultural stereotype; in thinking that it is really possible for a 'conditioned imagination' to actually see Friday as simply a 'fellow-being'. He will be shown to be human — as Shylock and Othello are human; but he will cease to be himself if he were to be seen as no more than human. Indeed, a realistic — as opposed to a sentimental — view of him would demand that his otherness be acknowledged and even made prominent. In other words, then, Friday is bound to be more than a slave; he has to be *the* slave, both by the accident of his having been actually enslaved and by the other and larger accident of being outside Crusoe's (and Defoe's) civilisation.

This leads to a further matter of some interest, namely, that *Robinson Crusoe* could not have led the reader to this conclusion were it not for the fact that the savage hero lends himself only too naturally to dramatisation as loyal slave. Thus when he is enslaved, he is not shown as a man denied liberty but as one only too glad, like the faithful dog, to serve a master. In *Robinson Crusoe*, as a result, the enslavement of Man Friday is made to look like a simple natural event. Crusoe finds that he can enslave Xury and Man Friday without having to take the moral responsibility for the act. It falls on the two savages to offer their services loyally and completely to their new master. Crusoe's part of the contract is to be kind and considerate to them. And he keeps it.

After he had thrown his Moorish companion overboard during a fishing trip, Crusoe was undecided what to do with the young boy, Xury, who was with him. The Moor, indeed, had sought Crusoe's mercy by pledging that 'he would go all over the world with [Crusoe]'. 'I could ha' been content to ha' taken this Moor with me and ha' drowned the boy,' Crusoe says, 'but there was no venturing to trust him.' Thus, in principle, the Moor was prepared to serve Crusoe; only Crusoe's caution prevented him from accepting the offer. Crusoe then turned to Xury and asked him to swear allegiance to him. Xury does so, not out of fear, as one would expect, but out of an instinctive willingness to be the servant. 'The boy smiled in my face, and spoke so innocently that I could not mistrust him; and swore to be faithful to me and go all over the world with me.'[24] A 'cordial and friendly' relationship was thereby established. Crusoe was the master, Xury the servant, and the acceptance of this distribution of roles was the condition for friendship. Even then, Crusoe felt no scruples in selling Xury to a Portuguese trader for sixty pieces of silver.

Defoe prepares us for the 'friendship' of Crusoe and Friday with more care. One of the first thoughts that occurred to Crusoe as he considered means of escaping from his confinement was the capture of a savage: 'if possible, it should be one of their prisoners who they had condemned to be eaten and should bring him hither to kill.'[25] He elaborated this thought into a scheme to obtain two or three savages 'so as to make them entirely slaves to me, to do whatever I should direct them.'[26] When he found Friday running towards his camp, Crusoe was at first frightened. But he immediately realised that 'part of my dream was coming to pass, and that [Friday] would certainly take shelter in my grove. . . . It came now very warmly upon my thoughts, and indeed irresistibly, that now was the time to get me a servant, and perhaps a companion, or assistant; and that I was called

plainly by Providence to save this poor creature's life.'[27]
Having saved Friday's life, Crusoe tells us that Friday spon-
taneously resolved to be his slave for life:

> . . . he came nearer and nearer, kneeling down every ten or
> twelve steps, in token of acknowledgement for my saving
> his life. I smiled at him and looked pleasantly, and
> beckoned to him to come still nearer; at length he came
> close to me; and then he kneeled down again, kissed the
> ground, and laid his head upon the ground, and taking me
> by the foot, set my foot upon his head; this, it seems, was
> in token of swearing to be my slave for ever.[28]

Friday gives this token of subjection to Crusoe several times
in the novel, always laying himself prostrate 'with all the
possible signs of an humble, thankful disposition, making a
great many antic gestures to show it.' Crusoe thus saw
himself as left with no option but to make Friday his slave. 'I
likewise taught him to say Master, and then let him know
that was to be my name.'[29]
    Friday's willingness to be a slave takes away from Crusoe
the moral responsibility for the enslavement. The psycho-
logical appropriateness of the loyal savage stereotype thus
eliminates what would have been a dishonest rationalisation
of slave-dealing on Crusoe's part. Between Crusoe and Friday
there developed the only possible relationship in their context: the relationship of master and slave. As Crusoe tells us,
'never man had a more faithful loving sincere servant than
Friday was to me; without passions, sullenness, of designs,
perfectly obliged and engaged; his very affections were tied
to me, *like those of a child to a father*.'[30] What we have here
is clearly a return to the archetypal situation in *The Tempest*
where Caliban worships the worthless Stephano and Trinculo
as gods. One difference is that Crusoe's situation lacks the
moral certainty of Shakespeare's play. A more important
difference is that Defoe's uncertain imaginative disposition

excludes the possibility of that comic reversal of roles which enabled Shakespeare to mock both savage and European in his play.[3][1]

We should notice here that in his characterisation of Friday as servant, Defoe does not compare him with the European servant because Friday is not the servant but the savage slave stereotype. This means that Friday's loyalty to Crusoe is not of the same kind as that of — say — an English housekeeper, again because the relationship which develops between the European and the savage servant can have no true equivalent in European society. It is, again, *sui generis*. In a European context, Friday's kind of loyalty and goodness would have appeared unmanly, even degrading and could never have earned him the admiration or affection of the reader. In Man Friday, however, these qualities become virtues because there is a disposition at work which thinks highly of Friday on account of his natural and uncomplicated eagerness to be a loyal slave.

It is possible, at this point, to generalise, and say that as long as the savage hero is playing a role such as that of the loyal slave, for which there are no possible European parallels, he remains a plausible character. On the other hand, whenever his role implies comparisons with the values of Europe, when, for example, his morality is compared to that of Europeans, it becomes immediately difficult for the imagination of Europe to believe in the nobility of the savage hero. For example, when Defoe tries to argue that anthropophagy may perhaps be acceptable to the natural morality of the Caribs, that these cannibals were no worse than the Christians who 'put whole troops of men to the sword', we begin to suspect, even from the rhetorical exaggeration of the phrasing, that he is straining to make a point and that he is being sentimental about it. In other words, we lack the disposition to accept the natural virtue of the Negro character when to do so would imply a comment on the relative quality of morality in Europe and Africa. Only when the

Negro character is treated in complete isolation from the morality of Europe are we likely to accept the values attributed to him as genuine. We would otherwise feel that these attributes have been ascribed to him only to be used as a criticism of the values of Christian Europe. Thus, even when Defoe recognises that savages have 'the same powers, the same reason, the same affections, the same sentiments of kindness and obligation, the same passions and resentments of wrongs, the same sense of gratitude, sincerity, fidelity, and all the capacities of doing and receiving good, that he has given to us',[32] he does not show how this is true of the Indians he describes in his novel. Only Man Friday and his father are represented as having any of these faculties, and even then only in a limited way. The savage hero is thus isolated not only from Europe but from his fellow savages. The extent to which Defoe can celebrate his savage hero turns out to have been determined not by his imaginative abilities nor by his personal sympathies as such, but by the disposition of the imagination of his civilisation and his age to accept his celebration as justifiable.

In *Oroonoko, or the Royal slave*, Mrs Aphra Behn tries to contrast the standards of conduct of the African prince with that of his European captors. The result is a glaring incongruity between the figure presented to us and the sentiments we are expected to believe him to have. Oroonoko had given his word to the captain of the ship that he would 'behave himself in all friendly Order and Manner, and obey the command of the Captain.' But the Captain would not trust his sincerity. This outrages Oroonoko: '*Oroonoko* then reply'd. He was very sorry to hear that the Captain pretended to the Knowledge and Worship of any Gods, who had taught him no better Principles, than not to credit as he would be credited.' Differences in religion, he argues, should not occasion distrust. Moreover the captain was swearing by the name of his God who would punish with the torments of hell. Oroonoko considers this less onerous than his oath on his own Honour:

> 'Which to violate, would not only render me contemptible
> and despised by all brave and honest Men, and so give my
> self perpetual Pain, but it would be eternally offending and
> displeasing all Mankind; harming, betraying, circum-
> venting, and outraging all Men ... I speak not this to move
> Belief, but to shew you how you mistake, when you
> imagine, that he who will violate his Honour, will keep his
> Word with the Gods.' So, turning from him with a
> disdainful smile, he refused to answer him.[33]

When the ship arrives at the island, Oroonoko offered no
resistance but only 'beheld the Captain with a Look all fierce
and disdain, upbraiding him with Eyes that forc'd Blushes on
his guilty Cheeks, he only cry'd in passing over the side of the
ship: *Farewell, Sir, 'tis worth my suffering to gain so true a
Knowledge, both of you* and of your Gods, by whom you
swear.'[34] Mrs Behn does nothing more here than embarrass
her fellow Europeans by presenting this holy savage. She even
does this at the expense of Oroonoko who, like the other
noble savages of the literature of the anti-slavery movement,
lived one grand operatic existence. Like the other savage
heroes of the age, Oroonoko does not arouse understanding;
only astonishment. It is indicative of the inherent confusion
in Mrs Aphra Behn's outlook and in that of those who
adapted her novel for the stage, that Oroonoko becomes so
respectable on the island that his values become those of
Europe and Christianity. Repenting himself of his part in the
attempted slave revolt on the island, Oroonoko, in a very
revealing speech, admits the folly of the enterprise:

> a whitely shame
> To think I could design to make those free
> Who were by nature slaves; wretches design'd
> To be their master's dogs, and lick their feet.

Whip, whip 'em to the knowledge of your gods,
Your Christian gods, . . .
I would not live on the same earth with creatures,
That only have faces of their kind;
Why should they look like men, who are not so? . . .
I wish they had their tails.[35]

Oroonoko's speech brings to the surface a current of thought and belief with which Mrs Aphra Behn and the other writers of the period had refused to come to terms. In this speech, the primary and authentic attitudes of the century came to the fore; the objections to the appearance of the negro, the assumption that he is a natural dog and slave and the feeling that only Christianity could emancipate him from his pagan barbarism. These attitudes are given expression through a symbol drawn from one of the oldest eighteenth-century traditions of the negro: that of the orang outang: 'I wish they had their tails.' Monboddo had argued:

Those who have not studied the variety of nature in animals, and particularly in man, the most various of all animals, will think this story, of men with tails, very ridiculous; and will laugh at the credulity of the author for seeming to believe such stories; But the philosopher, who is more disposed to inquire than to laugh and deride, will not reject it at once, as a thing incredible, that there should be such a variety in our species, as well as in the simian tribe, which is so near kin to us.[36]

One pointer to the fundamental character of the imaginative conditioning of the Enlightenment is the fact that in spite of the philosophers of primitivism so-called and the humanitarian enthusiasm of the emancipationists, the age-old stereotypes of the savage hero persisted throughout the century. Our argument is that English literature of the Enlightenment could have produced powerful images of the so-called savage hero if it had had the courage to eschew the superficial sentiments with which it obscured its deeper and more authentic attitudes towards the African and the Indian.

There is an important connection here with the emergence of the so-called 'Good Jew' in English literature of this period. For if we acknowledge the importance of the exo-cultural hero as a stereotype, we come to understand why the same compromised imagination which made a sentimental and silly hero of the African and the Indian also turned the thrifty, usurious and heartless Jew of Elizabethan drama into the tender imbecile of English Restoration and later drama. In fact with the saintly Jew, the English dramatists and novelists, especially Cumberland and Edgeworth, were self-consciously anxious to make amends. In his *Memoirs*, Richard Cumberland explains that he looked into society 'for the purpose of discovering such as were the victims of national, professional or religious prejudices; in short, those suffering characters which stood in need of an advocate'. Out of these, Cumberland notes, 'I meditated to select and form heroes for my future dramas of which I would study to make such favourable and reconciliatory delineations, as might include the spectators to look upon them with pity and receive them with good opinion and esteem.'[37] His Jewish characters were therefore seen as a different category of people from the audience, and were accordingly the proper object for pity and sympathy. Whereas the Elizabethan Jew was seen as an alien who could only be incorporated into Elizabethan society by the simple but fundamental act of formal baptism — that is, a conversion into Christianity — the eighteenth-century Jew was expected to win acceptance for himself by the total rejection of what the period took to be his nature. In other words, such a character had to satisfy his audience that he had rejected the known characteristics of his type. He had to be kind and gentle and represent the very opposite of what his Jewish being was thought to profess. Hence, as Edgar Rosenberg says, a myth was created to disprove a myth.[38] The good Jew of the eighteenth-century may then be said to be a deliberate construct to counteract the original myth of the anti-Christian Jew.

The important point, of course, is that if the Jew of Cumberland's drama is a kind of professional do-gooder and a sentimental creature, it is because the imaginative response of the audience to him can only be one of wonder at a spectacular variant of the Jewish norm. Because the audience cannot sincerely believe in the new construct, its attitude remains intellectually viable but emotionally unsatisfactory. The effect is sentimentalism because even Cumberland's hero, Sheva, is an elderly Israelite, a non-Christian, a money-lender, who is persecuted but wealthy; he is brutal in his treatment of his servant; he spends nothing on himself. The differences are also significant. He helps the weak; lends money gratis to Frederick, settles large sums of money on the penniless Eliza and appoints Eliza's suitor heir to his property. Thus, on his own accord, he carries out those same obligations that Shylock had been forced by the Venetian court to undertake. As Rosenberg puts it 'Behind Shylock's mask lies the reality of Sheva.'[39]

But Rosenberg deals with the problem as if it was entirely one of dramatic conventions. He argues that unlike the Jew villain the conditions for the good Jew were not religious; 'no mean mass superstitions cling to him and he cannot be explained in terms of profound collective motives and neuroses. He emerged in the drama of the Enlightenment brought forth in a spirit of tolerance tempered by sentimentality.'[40] The last phrase is misleading. The good Jew is sentimental because he is a deliberate attempt to eliminate the conditioned imagination; because he is the result of an attempt (which in the circumstances, was bound to fail) to deny the necessarily exo-cultural nature of the Jew stereotype in European literature.

5 Conrad's Nigger

André Gide tells us that on his third visit to the Congo Rapids, he was able to cross one of the branches of the River Djou and come 'right up to the banks of the big river', where

> the height of the waves and the impetuosity of the current can be seen particularly well. The sky set its serene and radiant seal upon a spectacle that was more majestic than romantic. From time to time an eddy churns up the water; a jet of foam leaps up. There is no rhythm; and I cannot understand these irregularities in the current.[1]

When one of the guests remarked that it was incredible that 'a spectacle like this is still without its painter', Gide's reaction is an unspoken entry in his diary.

> This is an invitation to which I shall not respond. The quality of temperance is an essential one in art, and enormity is repugnant to it. A description is none the more moving because ten is put instead of one ... it is a common mistake to suppose that the sublimity of a picture depends on the enormity of its subject.[2]

Since Gide dedicated his *Travels* to Conrad, it is hardly surprising that this spectacle should remind him of his fellow-traveller of the Congo. But in this particular instance, Gide was thinking, not of Conrad's *Heart of Darkness* but of *Typhoon*, a novel in which, according to him, Conrad seems to 'have done admirably in cutting short his story just on the threshold of the horrible and in giving the reader's imagination full play, after having led him to a degree of dreadfulness that seemed impossible.'³ The compliment is important, because the restraint which Gide commends is one which a writer is hardly ever able to achieve when his subject is exo-cultural; when, that is, the audience has a strong culturally-derived attitude to the fictional subject. Hence in spite of himself, Gide loses that 'quality of restraint' in dealing with the 'mysterious' and 'exotic' world of Africa which he had commended in the Conrad of *Typhoon*. He writes:

> I have plunged into this journey like Curtius into the gulf; [a journey] imposed upon me by a sort of ineluctable fatality ... what joy to find oneself among Negroes! ... On the wharf a swarm of Negroes hurry about like black ants, pushing trucks before them ... naked Negroes run about, shouting, laughing, quarreling, and showing their cannibal teeth ... they will be brought back again on the return voyage. Admirable men for the most part but we shall only see them again with their clothes on.

And: 'The natives' *indiscretion* can no doubt be explained by their *want of reserve*: one offers them a cigarette — they take the whole packet; a cake on a dish and they take the whole dish.'⁴

In the same breath, Gide speaks of the 'rapture' with which he reread La Fontaine's fables. 'I can hardly think of a single quality he does not possess ... his touch is often so slight and so delicate. He is a miracle of culture.'⁵ Such delicacy would have been inappropriate to a subject as alien as the Congo. Hence Gide finds himself in the absurdly ironic situation in which to lack restraint and to be indelicate is to be cultured.

A similar lack of restraint is evident in Conrad's *Nigger of the 'Narcissus'*, a novel that deals with an exo-cultural character. In the novels that preceded *The Nigger of the 'Narcissus'*, Conrad counted too much on the evocative language of his fiction to establish both the facts of his story and the emotional attitude he expected his audience to attach to these situations. In *Almayer's Folly*, for instance, Conrad's adjectives, as Newhouse says, 'insist too protestingly and the highly artifical rhythm strains too much'.[6] H. G. Wells drew attention to the same problem in his review of *An Outcast*: 'Mr Conrad is wordy. He has still to learn the great half of his art, the art of leaving things unwritten.'[7] The triumph of the *Typhoon* from this point of view is, as Gide has mentioned, in Conrad's reticence; his realisation that a description is not the more impressive because 'ten is put instead of one'. Moreover, Conrad depended on the exotic setting of his novels and the unique experiences of his characters for the success of his fiction. In situations, therefore, where exaggeration and novelty are only partially appropriate, Conrad's prose gives the definite impression of straining hard at producing an effect; the emotions intended by the language of his work do not in any way correspond to those proposed by the author. In other situations, such as that of *The Nigger of the 'Narcissus'*, though the prose is the same, the strain is thought not to exist because the subject is exo-cultural.

In his review of recent approaches to the interpretation of Conrad's *The Nigger of the 'Narcissus'*, Ian Watt has condemned the tendency to read symbolic meanings into the character of James Wait, the Negro character of this novel. He does admit that Wait is a special kind of character whose 'portentous first appearance, and the way he later becomes the chief protagonist round whom the actions and the attitudes of the crew revolve . . . certainly justify our impulse to look for some hidden significance in him'.[8] What he objects to is the kind of symbol-hunting represented, for example, by the writings of Vernon Young and of James E. Miller who, in particular, claims that James Wait and the sea are 'symbols of death and life'.[9] Ian Watt says of this argument that it is a 'confessedly simplified paradigm'.

> Surely no one would have seized upon the particular pattern if he had not, in the first place, felt sure that there must be some such neat symbolic plot waiting to be discovered, and in the second, felt justified in giving decisive interpretative priority to a few selected details of character and incident which could be made to support it (p. 267).

Ian Watt similarly rejects Young's account, which, he says, 'reveals a very Galahad of the symbol' (p. 268). Conrad's story, Watt contends, cannot be schematised as if it were some allegorical drama.

Watt's argument is a theoretical one. It holds that the weakness in symbol-hunting lies in the fact that the hunters are seeking what he terms *heterophoric* rather than *homeophoric* symbols:

> The basic problem is to determine the kind of relationship between the literary symbol and its referent, between the narrative vehicle and its imputed larger tenor; most important, perhaps, are the distances between them and the basis on which the mutual rapport is ascribed. In the kind of interpretation I have been considering, the distance between the literary object and the symbolic meaning ascribed to it is rather great: and so I would describe making Wait a symbol of evil or Satan, an example of *heterophoric* interpretation, that is, it carries us to another meaning, it takes us beyond any demonstrable connection between the literary object and the symbolic meaning given to it (p. 272).

In so far, at least, as it concerns *The Nigger of the 'Narcissus'*, this distinction is a very important but also a possibly

misleading one. It warns us, rightly enough, against too
fanciful a reading of the novel. But it also seems to imply
that Wait's symbolic equivalent can be determined in the
same way that, for example, we can arrive at the symbolic
function of Shakespeare's Angelo, which is, in fact, not true.
The problem, for this novel and others like it, ought really to
be stated in other terms. For the difficulty is how to describe
the reader's reaction to the presence of the black hero
without appearing to be imposing categories on the novel. In
the criticism of a Miracle or a Morality play, it is appropriate
to speak of the symbols of Vice and Grace, of Death and
Salvation, of Devils and Angels. In those cases, the form of
the drama which operates outside the realm of character and
personality and concentrates on that of signification and
idea, *requires* such an approach. It is in this sense, after all,
that these figures come to be thought of as abstractions, and
the modification of their form in characters like Shakespeare's Angelo to be seen as symbolic. That is to say, we can
talk of a character in a morality play (or in plays that quite
evidently exist under its inspiration) as being symbolic, in
both the *hetero* and the *homeophoric* senses, without violence or injustice to the true meaning of the work.

In *The Nigger of the 'Narcissus'*, however, the immediate
physical reality of Wait is so prominent that the search for a
symbolic equivalent for his role leads to two possibilities:
Wait is either symbol enough in himself or we must find some
extravagant categories for aspects of an existing reality. Thus,
when Harold E. Davis says that Wait is 'equated with the
devil, a "black idol", the prince of darkness, the tortured and
dark areas of experience through which all men must pass to
arrive at certainty',[10] we are not sure whether he means this
as a symbolic analysis of the novel or is merely writing a
metaphorical description of the literal experience of the
story.

Watt calls a procedure such as Davis's a 'reductio ad
symbolum' (p. 267). The rejection of this method should

not, however, be combined with a refusal to deal with the
fact that Conrad's treatment of Wait is, to say the least,
unique. Ian Watt concedes that much, though he cites
Conrad's antipathy to Melville, and Conrad's 1914 note 'To
My Readers in America' to explain away the importance of
this black hero. 'Conrad does not, in Melville's sense, believe
in any absolute or transcendental "evil" and his Negro has
not done any' (p. 270). Conrad's 1914 note categorically
denies Wait: 'In the book (Wait) is nothing; he is merely the
ship's collective psychology and the pivot of the action. . . .'
The conclusion to draw from both of these comments — and
Watt does not try to do so — is that Wait may well be a
symbol in a more obvious and immediate sense than he or the
symbol-hunters have imagined. This chapter seeks to explore
this possibility, and thereby to redefine both the character of
the black hero and the implications of the characterisation
not only for Conrad's readers but for his novel, too.

The problem can perhaps be seen from a better angle if,
for a moment, we reflect on the function of Queequeg in
Melville's *Moby Dick*. Whatever else he may be, Queequeg is
offered as a very sharp contrast — in his person and his
background — to the 'European'[11] and Christian part of the
Pequod crew. He has a function essential to the theme and
symbolic meaning of the novel. This function, however, is
not arbitrary. It was not left absolutely to Melville to
determine what it was to be; nor could it have been
performed adequately by any of the regular American members of the crew. Moreover, Queequeg performs this function
not in an individual capacity, as a person with experiences
and attitudes all his own, but as a representative figure, a firm
pagan counterpart to the Christian culture of the world of
Melville and of the novel. We may, as readers, feel that we
know Queequeg as well as we would ever want to. In fact,
however, the individual, the inner man in Queequeg is not
there; he is beyond us. What appears in Melville's novel is
mainly an instrument of Melville's criticism. His racial fea-

tures, the expectations of the reader and the thwarting of those expectations — these are the character of his savage. In performing this role, then, Queequeg depends on his exocultural personality and background. In fact, much of the meaning of the novel depends on our appreciating that Ishmael ultimately finds more companionship and even brotherhood in that frightful-looking savage than in the world of civilised men which he rejected at the opening of the novel. Ishmael's first meeting with Queequeg is intended to establish an initial *physical* revulsion on Ishmael's part from the man who later was to be his friend and saviour. Ishmael records this initial shock: 'Good heavens! what a sight! Such a face! It was of a dark, purplish, yellow color, here and there stuck over with large, blackish looking squares.'[1] [2] Part of Ishmael's problem is one of ignorance:

> Ignorance is the parent of fear, and being completely nonplussed and confounded about the stranger, I confess I was as much afraid of him as if it was the devil himself who had thus broken into my room at the dead of night. In fact, I was so afraid of him that I was not game enough just then to address him, and demand a satisfactory answer concerning what seems inexplicable in him (p. 38).

What Ishmael in this ignorance imagines to be a devil's mask is in fact a man's face, Queequeg's *usual face*. That face was repulsive, first to Ishmael and subsequently, by a natural and reasonable extension, to Melville's readers. Or more exactly, Melville's readers would be expected to accept Ishmael's feelings of revulsion as justified. A critic could easily extract the comparison of Queequeg with the devil and construct from it a scheme of allegorical meanings. That would be particularly unnecessary if we realise that the comparison is not some ingenious discovery on Melville's part but a manner of words as naturally appropriate in European circles to Queequeg's appearance as calling a black man 'monkey' or, as in Elizabethan times, 'devil'. Melville is simply placing what turns out to be Queequeg's inner 'goodness' besides the 'devilishness' with which, on the basis of traditional associations, Queequeg is ordinarily connected. Queequeg can function satisfactorily as an ironic symbol of primitive goodness because Melville makes him the reversal of the obviously symbolic expectations of the audience from such a savage. Melville lets him operate essentially in a context in which he will constitute a permanent criticism of the civilised and hypocritical society of New England. In this sense, then, Watt is right in contrasting Melville's and Conrad's use of 'blackness' as symbol.

James Wait is in a similar predicament, though Conrad does not use him for the same fulfilment of any transcendental purposes similar to Melville's. Conrad presents his main character not as a *sick sailor* but as a *repulsive blackman*. Conrad plays on Wait's negroid features and (as it were) celebrates them to the point where they become not merely descriptions of the man, but an epitome of his nature. The man ceases, or rather, is subsumed in the Negro identity which Conrad has created for him. Wait is, thus, symbolic not in the ordinary sense that Conrad set him up to represent an abstract idea, but in the special sense that Conrad asserts a correspondence (Melville subverts this correspondence) between the imaginative predispositions of his European audience to this black sailor and his realised role in the novel. And, quite as importantly, Conrad does it by appearing to write entirely on the realistic plane. Where Melville treats the man as if he were a myth, Conrad treats the myth and the man as one.

Another comparison may be made, this time with Burns of Conrad's *The Shadow Line* who, like Wait, has been described as one of Conrad's 'Jonahs'. According to Frederick J. Masback 'both men appear . . . as an interruption of the established order and tranquility of the ship, causing a distinct sense of discomfort and even shock by their sudden appearance, and their surly and evasive attitude.'[13] Harold E. Davis comments: 'The pilgrimage scene is the basic pattern in the novel and it is this theme which is largely carried by the complex symbolism. Into the world of the *Narcissus* comes Wait, a black, diseased fear, unknowable and thus more powerful, sowing dissension and violence.'[14] The comparisons with Burns and the reference to the pilgrimage theme are a hindrance rather than an aid to the understanding of the different roles which Wait and Burns play in the two novels. In the first place, of course, *The Nigger of the 'Narcissus'* is not concerned principally with the fact of a pilgrimage, although, in some sense, every sea journey which involves a struggle with the elements is a kind of pilgrimage. For another, Conrad does not characterise Wait and Burns in the same way. In *The Shadow Line*, Burns is an embittered man. As Conrad tells us, he had hoped to attain the mastership of the boat, but had been unfortunately disappointed in that hope. 'He took the ship to a point where he expected to be confirmed in his temporary command from lack of a qualified master to put over his head.'[15] We are not told this till late in the story, but we are expected to make use of this information in re-evaluating our impressions of him from the early scenes where we were made to feel that his malice is an irrational objection to the new captain. The captain had then complained of Burns' 'long, red moustache [which] determined the character of his physiognomy'. This physiognomy, he tells us, 'struck me as pugnacious in (strange to say) a ghastly sort of way' (p. 77). The qualifying parenthesis is an important clue to what Conrad intended us to feel about the narrator himself. It asks us to withhold our conclusion, and to accept that this physical appearance, 'the long, red moustache', did not have an intrinsic connection with a pugnacious personality. The comparison is therefore a momentary, almost whimsical one, and Conrad saw that he could not depend exclusively on Burn's physiognomy for the establishment of his character. With Wait, as we shall see, the emphasis is different: his features had an intrinsic association.

Burns has also been described as 'repulsive', and this can be misleading if we do not pay close attention to how Conrad describes the man. Burns is more a man with hard and severe features than one who is, himself, repulsive. 'His face in the full light of day appeared pale, meagre, even haggard. Somehow I had a delicacy as to looking too often at him; his eyes, on the contrary, remained fairly glued to my face. They were greenish and had an expectant expression' (p. 78). Even as he is about to die from sickness, Burns, though emaciated, is not despicable. Conrad does not describe him with any hints of revulsion. Instead he returns to the *facts* of his condition and to a repetition of his earlier comments on his character. Conrad thus refers to 'the preternatural sharpness of the ridge of his nose, the deep cavities of his temples'. 'He was so reduced that he would probably die very soon' (p. 136). In a final summing up of the man, Conrad tells us that Burns 'feared neither God, nor devil, nor man, nor wind, nor his own conscience. And I believe he hated everybody and everything. But I think he was afraid to die' (p. 138).

Burns, then, is a human being. His influence on the ship and on the captain can be established in terms of character and spiritual decadence. He is a temptation to the captain, who almost yields to Burn's fear that the spirit of the former captain, now dead, hovers over the ship, and that this spirit is really responsible for the dead calm. As he stumbles over Burns on all fours, the captain thinks he has seen the alleged ghost, 'that thing!' This fall is a symbolic act: a wind arises and the ship is on its way again.

Two points are worth noting here. The first is that though both Wait and Burns seem to call forth the storm and the calm plaguing their ships, the relationship of Burns to his story differs from that of Wait to his. James Wait has no personal history such as Burns has to account for his influence on the voyage. Burns is a tempter to the young captain; he is a positive character. Wait is not: his impact on the crew comes from the qualities with which the crew themselves invest him.

The other point is that Burn's story is a personal, even humane, story in a way that Wait's is not. We do not approve of Burn's moral position, but we understand why a man with his background can be thus deranged. His malady and his satanism have a human explanation. In *The Nigger of the 'Narcissus'*, Wait comes on board with his illness and his physical appearance, and both forces — the first augmenting the second — work the magic of his charm on the crew. Wait, as Conrad said, is nothing. He has no background, no being, no projected self. He is an enigma, a powerful portent. That portentous power derives from the combination in him of his negroid features, as these are seen by Conrad (or his fictional narrator), and the terror which is assumed to accompany these features.

It is the argument of this chapter, then, that the symbolic power of Wait's blackness is not a metaphorical construct but a kind of brutal fact to which Conrad draws attention in the story. In the characterisation of Burns (as well, incidentally, as in Melville's characterisation of Jackson in *Redburn*), the satanism of character is shown in terms of deformation of the body or face. Burns is haggard and skinny just before his death. Melville's Jackson had nothing left of him 'but the foul lees and dregs of a man; he was thin as a shadow; nothing but skin and bones; and sometimes used to complain that it hurt him to sit on the hard chests.'[16] In *The Nigger of the 'Narcissus'*, Wait is also sick and emaciated but his repulsive appearance is not described in terms of this condition, but of his racial appearance which his illness only heightens. Conrad makes this clear at the opening of the novel, when it is not a *sickly* but a *black* man that arrests the attention of the crew: 'The boy, amazed like the rest, raised the light to the man's face. It was black. A surprised hum — a faint hum that sounded like the suppressed mutter of the word "Nigger" — ran along the deck and escaped out into the night.[1][7] In other words, the fact that Wait is a nigger had, in itself, a magical effect on the ship even before the crew came to know of his illness. Against this background of suppressed consternation, Conrad formally introduces James Wait as 'calm, cool, towering, superb'.

> He overtopped the tallest by a half a head ... The deep-ruling tones of his voice filled the deck without effort. He was naturally, scornfully, unaffectedly condescending, as if from his height of six foot three he had surveyed all the vastness of human folly and had made up his mind not to be too hard on it ... he stood still surrounded by all these white men (pp. 34—5).

Conrad's tone here is difficult to determine since it is not clear whether he is speaking as detached — and therefore impartial — observer, or as one of the already excited crew. In the latter case, his comment would be a projection of his fear. Whether, however, Conrad is being frank or ironic, the effect of the description is to introduce Wait as the mighty and somewhat incongruous opposite to the rest of the crew. In sum, Wait's power over the crew, hinted at in their suppressed shudder on seeing his face, is paralleled by his physical tyranny over them.

Having established these points, Conrad turns more carefully to the details of Wait's physique, to the source of his power. Held up in the glare of a lamp, Wait's head is seen as being: 'vigorously modelled into deep shadows and shinning lights — a head powerful and misshapen with a tormented and flattened face — a face pathetic and brutal: the tragic, the mysterious, the repulsive mask of a nigger's soul' (p. 35).[1][8] The sentence says many things. Stylistically, it is a tortured effort — notice the clausal breaks — to realise a difficult fact. More, the sentence draws a sharp and very important contrast between the nigger's appearance and his soul, though it does not say that this soul is any more pleasant than the mask. At any rate, it is the 'mask', the appearance, that is described as 'repulsive'. This is no compliment to Wait, of course. But it does establish that Conrad felt the distinction important, that he found in the negro features of Wait the heart of his mystery. It is Wait's blackness and this includes his negroid features in their natural, not their distorted, form, that is his chief 'attraction'. In his colour and his features he carried almost all his magic.

Wait is inscrutable: 'You couldn't see that there was anything wrong with him: a nigger doesn't show' (p. 51). His very presence seemed to be the antithesis of light. When at one point in the story he comes on deck, he

> seemed to hasten the retreat of a departing light by his very presence; the setting sun dipped sharply as though fleeing before our nigger; a black mist emanated from him; a subtle and dismal influence; a something cold and gloomy that floated out and settled on all the faces like a mourning veil. The circle broke up. The joy of laughter died on stiffened lips. There was not a smile left among the ship's company. Not a word was spoken (p. 45).

Conrad returns to this comparison several times in the novel. In one passage written obviously for effect but otherwise not an isolated purple passage, Conrad recreates what beyond doubt was the exotic but weird attraction he found in Wait's colour:

> When the light was put out, and through the door thrown wide open, Jimmy, turning on his pillow, could see vanishing beyond the straight line of top-gallant rail, the quick repeated visions of a fabulous world made up of leaping fire and sleeping water. The lightning gleamed in his black face, and then he would lie blinded and invisible in the midst of an intense darkness (p. 89).

Because they are so conspicuous, these references to Wait's *colour* have been extracted and fitted into ready categories by critics who only see his colour as the abstract signal of symbolic meaning. Wait's physical appearance has not been similarly taken into account, even though the text makes it clear that Conrad saw Wait's physiognomy as another aspect of his Negro personality. Conrad continually refers to Wait's eyes, for example, as 'bulging', 'startlingly prominent', 'staring', and rolling 'wildly'. Conrad does this with an insistence that makes it evident that he is not referring to these eyes as an idiosyncratic feature of Wait's but as a natural phenomenon — quite clearly non-European — which he finds distracting and even disgusting. Apart from these eyes, Conrad also comments on Wait's lips: 'The lower lip hung down, enormous and heavy' (p. 68). 'His heavy lips protrude in an everlasting black pout' (p. 94). As Negro Wait had these physical features of nose, cheeks and lips. Conrad (that is, the novel's narrator) also found these features repulsive in themselves.

Wait's person is seen in sub-human terms. He is compared either to an animal or to a corpse: 'There was an aspect astounding and animal-like in the perfection of his expectant immobility — the unthinking stillness of a scared brute' (p. 98). Or again: 'He was becoming immaterial like an apparition; his cheekbones rose, the forehead slanted more; the face was all hollows, patches of shade; and the fleshless head resembled a disinherited black skull, filled with two restless globes of silver in the sockets of eyes. He was demoralizing' (p. 111). The same feeling emerges when the crew try to rescue Wait: 'with concealing absurd gestures, like a lot of drunken men embarrassed with a stolen corpse' they felt themselves tottering together 'on the very brink of eternity' (p. 68). Conrad (as narrator) and Donkin, alone, speak out their minds and call Wait 'a black-faced swine' (p. 52), and 'the black brute' (p. 68). The others, though they share these sentiments, do not try to express them. In their world, Wait is an uncomfortable companion, and they are both scornful and frightened of him. Wait's strength comes from this embarrassment on the part of the crew:

> They clustered around that moribund carcass, the fit emblem of their aspirations, and encouraging one another, they swayed, they tramped on one spot, shouting that they would not be put upon [p. 100]. Jimmy condescended to laugh. It cheered up everybody wonderfully [p. 91]. Had we (by an incredible hypothesis) undergone similar toil and trouble for an empty cask, that cask would have become as precious to us as Jimmy was. More precious, in fact, because we would have had no reason to hate the cask. And we hated James Wait [p. 69].

These contradictions in feeling are caused by the mysteriousness of Wait's person, and his presence in their midst. Wait is a symbol, if we like, not in an esoteric or technical sense, but in the obvious sense that he is virtually a devil among them, an outsider, an occult creature, wearing a black and repulsive mask which the crew is necessarily incapable of piercing. They indeed admit that 'the man's a man if he is black' (p. 100). They nevertheless know that they cannot treat Wait either kindly or rudely, like one of themselves, without evident self-consciousness. As Conrad put it, it was as though they 'had been overcivilized, and rotten, and without any knowledge of the meaning of life. [They] had the air of being initiated in some infamous mysteries' (pp. 111–12).

It is quite clear here that Conrad is depending for this presentation of Wait on a long-standing tradition of associating the black man with the brute, and of equating physical with moral blackness. This is deducible from the fact that there are virtually no distinctions made in Conrad's narrative between literal descriptions of Wait and symbolic applications of his repugnant and demoralising personality. Moreover, Conrad is not using his references to Wait's malignity to confirm or supplement any traits of character which he had shown the hero to possess. Wait's magic is the magic of mere presence. In the vigour with which he describes Wait's impact on the crew, in the association of Wait with darkness, Conrad means us to see the 'demoralising' consequence of this presence. The moral decadence which Burns and Jackson introduce into the worlds of their novels comes from their history and their character. It is not a projection of the fears of the crew. Burns and Jackson are physically distorted as a consequence of their moral degeneracy: there is a kind of sympathetic logic. With Wait, the facts are otherwise. His natural features, described as exotic and repulsive, assume the proportions of sinister omens.

If, however, our comparison is between this novel and Conrad's *The Black Mate*, instead of between it and either *The Heart of Darkness* or *Benito Cereno*, we realise how unimportant for our analysis of the novel are those categories of symbols which do not spring from a recognition of Wait's natural repulsiveness. Published posthumously in *Tales of Hearsay*[19] but written about 1884, *The Black Mate* is essentially a typical Conrad story depending on mystery and ritual. It is in many ways a trite story, but that Conrad chose to write it, and to write it the way he did around a single embarrassment, is very revealing of some of his dispositions. The centre of the short novel is Bunter, the·ship's mate. Bunter was apparently an exceptional sailor:

[He] was noticeable to them in the street from a great distance; and when in the morning he strode down the jetty to his ship, the lumpers and the dock labourers rolling their bales and trundling the cases of cargo on their handtrucks would remark to each other: Here's the black mate coming along (p. 85).

Bunter was not a black man, unfortunately. He only had

black hair; 'absolutely black, black as a raven's wing' (p. 86). Conrad (or his narrator) objects very seriously to his appellation:

> That was the name [black mate] they gave him, being a gross lot who could have no appreciation of the man's dignified bearing. And to call him black was the superficial impression of the ignorant.
>
> Of course, Mr Bunter, the mate of the *Sapphire*, was not black. He was no more black than you or I, and not certainly as white as any chief mate of a ship in the whole of the port of London. ... A man may have black hair without being a Dago (p. 86).

Conrad makes a distinction here between a casual blackness and an intrinsic one, and suggests further that being a Dago (and having black hair as well) was of the latter, intrinsic kind. A Dago, that is, might be called 'black' without unfairness. This, in the logic of the story, would be particularly important, since being called black had several associations. For example, to call Bunter black would be to fail to appreciate 'the man's dignified bearing'.

However that may be, Bunter found that he was looked upon, even in his boat, with suspicion. Indeed Bunter's own captain did not feel differently from the 'gross lot': 'If anyone were to tell Captain Johns that he — Bunter — had a tail, Johns would manage to get himself to believe the story in some mysterious manner' (p. 92). Bunter had to dye his hair white. Conrad comments: 'Those eyes that looked at you so steely, so fierce, and so fascinating out of the bush of a buccaneer's black hair, now had an innocent, almost boyish expression in their good-humoured brightness under those white eye-brows' (p. 116). As long as Bunter had his black hair, he was a kind of 'diabolic' figure on board. Conrad himself speaks of Bunter's 'usual stately deliberation, made sinister by the form of his jet-black eyebrows' (p. 92). The

Captain, even in his retirement, 'tries to tell the story of a black mate he once had, "a murderous, gentlemanly ruffian", with ravenblack hair which turned all white all at once in consequence of a manifestation from beyond the grave. An avenging apparition' (p. 120).

If we think Bunter's story is a *comic* parallel of the Wait story, we have to explain our reaction. It seems clear, though, that the comedy lies in the preposterous nature of the allegation being made, in the ludicrous nature of the whole issue. In other words, the images of death and ferociousness, the references to spirits and apparitions could not in themselves arouse any genuine feeling that Bunter is capable of being any image or symbol. For this reason, we transfer the absurdity of the comparisons from their object — Bunter — to the crew and the captain. Because Bunter is not black in any true sense of the word, we discount the possibility that he can be charged with being the agent of demons. Conrad is with us in this feeling. Wait, on the other hand, has no such salvation. He is black in a real sense and the equation of this blackness to devilishness is not as easily written off as the aberration of the crew or of the narrator. In Bunter's story, we are made to understand what is the truth and what is rumour in the narrative. The narrator allows us a glimpse into his own prejudices and thus enables us to judge his attitude to the story he is telling. In *The Nigger of the 'Narcissus'*, the narrator is outside the story, impersonal, though involved in the action. The degree of his involvement is not made clear, however. As a result, we do not even consider the possibility that we are perhaps dealing with an over-sensitive narrator. We are forced, accordingly, to assume that Conrad is speaking, as novelists do speak, through the narrator. That is, we do not qualify the exotic account of Wait's person by assuming that the whole story is the appraisal of the situation by just one of Conrad's characters, and not the most valid and general assessment of it. The result of all this is that Wait becomes an entirely mysterious person and we are in no position to verify stories about him, however strange they may be. Because of a limitation in point of view, there is an even greater limitation in our view of the hero.

Two implications seem inevitable in the light of the preceding discussion. The first is that we have to see Wait as an exo-cultural stereotype, a character who does not really belong to the ship and its world. Wait has a certain weird attractiveness about him, and it is this rather than the question of his individual character as a seaman, that concerns Conrad in the novel. Another way of phrasing this would be that Conrad found in Wait the antithesis of everything he expected of a sailor in his cultural context. To write a different story about Wait, Conrad would have had to adopt a totally different attitude to Wait's colour and his physiognomy. The symbol of evil and death which Wait is said to represent is merely the consequence of Conrad's supposedly factual description of an appearance which, to him, was literally brutal, tragic and sinister. If we must call Wait a devil, we must mean the name to be a measure of Conrad's revulsion from these aspects of Wait's physiognomy.

The second implication is related to the first. If we cannot accept a story about Bunter's devilishness because Conrad could not have meant us to take him seriously, we are really admitting that the real determinant of the symbolic relevance of a character is the imagination of the audience rather than the mere presence of those literary features usually associated with symbolism. Bunter cannot serve as a serious representation of anything because the man and his qualities, however we celebrate them, cannot sustain the serious meaning we intend them thereby to. Wait, it seems to me, serves such a symbolic function as is attributed to him because there is some disposition to accept the appropriateness of the equivalence which Conrad makes, because we have an appropriately conditioned imagination. This means, therefore, that when such spontaneous revulsion from the reality of Negro features does cease to appear correct, when, that is, any such *literary* expression of natural and correct revulsion should appear to us exaggerated, the reading and evaluation of the symbolic importance of Wait will suffer. The difference, very often, between tragedy and melodrama lies in the supporting system of belief, a concurring sensibility. No reading of *The Nigger of the 'Narcissus'* which does not begin with such a concurring attitude to Conrad's mystique of the black personality can escape being melodramatic. What sustains this novel, then, is not the assumed symbolic patterns to be found in it — whether they are *heterophoric* or *homeophoric* — but our concurrence with Conrad that his rites of colour and sin are also true, in the literal sense; our initial acceptance that Conrad's statement about Wait's face being the 'tragic, the mysterious, the repulsive mask of a nigger's soul' is not sheer nonsense. Because the conditioned imagination of Europe accepts Conrad's claim, the symbols are inevitable. Conrad's strength, in short, derives almost entirely from that of his exo-cultural hero.

Notes

CHAPTER 1

1 Jonathan Culler, *Structuralist Poetics: Structuralism, Linguistics and the Study of Literature* (London, 1975) p. 113.
2 Ibid., p. 114.
3 F. R. Leavis, *The Living Principle: English as a Discipline of Thought* (London, 1975) p. 47.
4 Pierre Guiraud, *Semiology*, tr. George Gross (London, 1975) p. 58.
5 Edgar Rosenberg, *From Shylock to Svengali: Jewish Stereotypes in English Literature* (Stanford, 1960) p. 43.
6 Irving Howe, *William Faulkner: A Critical Study* (New York, 1962) p. 123.
7 Quoted in Wylie Sypher, *Enlightened England: An Anthology of English Literature from Dryden to Blake* (New York, 1962) pp. 816—7.
8 *Sinclair Lewis: A Collection of Critical Essays*, ed. Mark Schorer (Englewood Cliff, N.J., 1962) p. 23.
9 Ibid., p. 24.
10 Ibid., p. 50.
11 Ibid., p. 21.
12 *Phaedrus* 245a. See *Plato's Phaedrus*, tr. R. Hackforth (Cambridge, 1952) pp. 57—9.
13 See, for example, A. Alvarez, 'Wallace Stevens: Platonic Poetry', *Stewards of Excellence: Studies in Modern English and American Poets* (New York, 1958); Delmore Schwartz, 'The Ultimate Plato with Picasso's Guitar', *Harvard Advocate*, CXXVII (Dec 1940), 11—16; and Doris L. Elder, 'The Meaning of Wallace Stevens' Two Themes', *Critical Quarterly*, 11, no. 2 (Summer 1969), 181—90.
14 *Collected Poems of Wallace Stevens* (New York, 1954) p. 175.
15 *The Language of Criticism* (London, 1966) p. 61.
16 *The Problem of Style* (Oxford, 1922) p. 15.
17 Ibid., p. 16.

18 *Johnson: Prose and Poetry*, selected by Mona Wilson (London, 1957) p. 491.

19 Quoted in Lois Whitney, *Primitivism and the Idea of Progress* (New York, 1934) p. 13.

20 *Treatise of Human Nature*, Book I (New York, 1962) p. 197.

21 'Red Leaves', *The Portable Faulkner*, ed. Malcolm Cowley (New York, 1954) p. 75.

22 *Faulkner in the University*, eds. Frederick L. Gwynn and Joseph L. Blotner (Charlottesville, 1959) pp. 8—9.

23 The other two faces ('vermilion' for anti-Christian Jew and 'betwixt white and yellow' for Moslem Arab) belonged to groups which, like the blacks, were associated with aspects of the character of the devil.

24 In *Ben Jonson: Works*, ed. C. H. Herford and P. and E. Simpson, vol. VII (Oxford, 1941) II. 143—7.

25 Ibid., II. 125—8. See also vol. X (1950) pp. 448ff.

26 *Complete Writings of William Blake*, ed. Geoffrey Keynes (London, 1966) p. 125.

27 J. Edwin Whitesell, 'Blake's "Little Black Boy",' *Explicator*, V (Apr 1947) item 42.

28 Ralph D. Eberly, 'Blake's "Little Black Boy",' *Explicator*, XV (Apr 1957) item 42.

29 John Lewis Longley Jr, *The Tragic Mask: A Study of Faulkner's Heroes* (Chapel Hill, 1963) p. 193.

30 Ibid., p. 192.

31 'You dont know what you are. And more than that, you wont never know. You'll live and you'll die and you wont never know.' *Light in August*, Penguin edn (London, 1973) p. 288. See also *Faulkner in the University*, p. 72.

32 Richard Chase, 'Faulkner's *Light in August*', in *Twentieth Century Interpretations of 'Light in August'*, ed. David L. Minter (Englewood Cliffs, N.J., 1969) p. 21.

33 Cleanth Brooks, *William Faulkner: The Yoknapatawpha Country* (New Haven, 1963) p. 51.

34 *Light in August*, pp. 337—8.

35 Ibid., p. 349.

36 Willis Wager, *American Literature: A World View* (London, 1969) p. 171.

37 'Delta Autumn', in *Go Down, Moses* (New York, 1942) p. 360.

38 Ibid., p. 361.

39 Ibid., p. 364.

40 Ibid., p. 363.

41 Cf. 'The Bear' in *Go Down, Moses*, p. 278: 'the whole South is cursed, and all of us who derive from it, whom it ever suckled, white and black.'

42 Faulkner (1973) p. 190.

43 See Fred B. Millett and Gerald E. Bentley, *The Art of the Drama* (New York, 1935) p. 204: 'Such social types as the parasite, the boastful soldier, the procurer and procuress, the slave girls of Greek and Roman comedy tend to disappear from the drama as they disappeared from the actual life from which the dramatist drew his material.'

CHAPTER 2

1 Irving Ribner, 'Marlowe and Shakespeare', *SQ*, XV (spring 1964), 44–9.

2 George I. Duthie, *Shakespeare* (London, 1951) p. 37.

3 In Geoffrey Bullough, *Narrative and Dramatic Sources of Shakespeare*, I (London, 1957) p. 472.

4 Quoted in Ribner, pp. 44–5, f.n.7.

5 *Shakespearean Comedy* (London, 1949) p. 127.

6 Bernard Grebanier, *The Truth About Shylock* (New York, 1959) p.x.

7 He points this out (p. 47) in connection with Abigail's 'conversion' where the Friar 'laments above all else the death of a seducible virgin'.

8 *The Jew of Malta*, ed. H. S. Bennett (London, 1930) I.ii.68ff.

9 See the interesting observation in *Il Pecorone* (Bullough, p. 472) on the Jew's reason for insisting on a pound for flesh: 'many merchants joined together in offering to pay the money, but the Jew would not have it, for he wished to commit this homicide in order to be able to say that he put to death the greatest of the Christian merchants.'

10 See Grebanier (1959) p. 19. Grebanier's book contains a wealth of relevant historical and related data on the Jew in European history.

11 W. M. Foley, 'Marriage', *Encyclopaedia of Religion and Ethics*, ed. James Hastings, I (New York, 1908) p. 133.

12 Grebanier, p. 19.

13 See Grebanier, p. 20.

14 Grebanier, p. 20.

15 In *Patrologia Cursus Completus*, ed. J. Migne (Paris, 1850)

LXXXVII, 481.

16 Ibid., p. 103. Cf. Shylock's reply in IV. i, to Portia's speech, on mercy: 'My deeds upon my head'.

17 See also *Patrologia Cursus Completus*, LXXXVII, 235: 'Quam Noah nuditatem, id est, passionem Christi, videns Cham, derisit, et Judae Christi mortem videntes subsannaverunt.'

18 E.g. Matt. xxvii: 26—31; Mark xv: 15—20, and John xix: 1—3.

19 A. W. Pollard, *English Miracle Plays* (Oxford, 1909) p. 33. The Catholic Liturgy still has traces of this interpretation of Good Friday. *'Oremus et pro perfidis Judaeis*: ut et ipsi agnoscant Jesum Christum Dominum nostrum.' At other points in this sequence, the priest says 'Flectamus genua' after the 'Oremus'. *The Missal* specifically states that after the prayer for the Jews, the 'Flectamus is omitted, and the clergy and the people do not kneel down'. After a few more prayers, there follows the *Reproaches* in which the Priest (representing God) speaks of his rejection by the Jews. 'Quia eduxi te de terra Aegypti: parasti crucem Salvatori tuo.' 'Popule meus, quid feci tibi? aut in quo contristavi te? responde mihi', etc.

20 H. Fisch, *The Dual Image: A Study of the Figure of the Jew in English Literature* (London, 1959) pp. 13—14.

21 Deut. xxiii: 19—20 'You shall not lend upon interest to your brother, interest on money, interest on victuals, interest on anything that is lent for interest. To a foreigner you may lend upon interest, but to your brother you shall not lend upon interest.' See also Grebanier, p. 78.

22 See J. L. E. Ortolan, *The History of Roman Law* (London, 1871) pp. 105—6.

23 Quoted in Grebanier, p. 79.

24 G. Friedlander, *Shakespeare and the Jew* (London, 1921) pp. 26—7.

25 Grebanier (p. 80) notes that this position was not changed until 1830 when 'moderate interest' was made permissible.

26 William of Auxerre is said to have found the prohibition 'even more rigorous than the commandment against murder: there is no exception to the law of usury, where it is on occasion even meritorious to kill.' See B. N. Nelson, *The Ideas of Usury* (Princeton, 1949) p. 13.

27 Allan Bloom points out in his *Shakespeare's Politics* (New York, 1964) p. 16, that the Jews in Venice were 'well-off and enjoyed the full protection of the law . . . Shylock's claim against Antonio rests entirely on that law.' Antonio himself takes pride in this fact in *Merchant*, III. iii. 26—31. All references are to J. Russell Brown's Arden edn (London, 1955).

28 See John Webster's *The White Devil* (1612) II. ii. 45—6: '. . . If there were Jews enough, so many Christians would not turn usurers.'

29 *The Jew of Malta*, I. i. 112—13; 103—4.

30 See Leah W. Wilkins, 'Shylock's Pound of Flesh and Laban's Sheep', *MLN*, LVII (1947) 28—30, and Norman Nathan's 'Shylock, Jacob and God's Judgment', *SQ*, I (Oct 1950) 255—9. They disagree with each other's conclusion. The explanation offered here differs from theirs.

31 See Beatrice D. Brown, 'Medieval Prototypes of Lorenzo and Jessica', *MLN*, XLIV (1929) 227—32.

32 Ribner misses this point completely. Jessica, he says (p. 48) 'is an agent of her father's redemption', forgetting apparently that Jessica and his gold were together all his life. E.g., III. i. 33. On the marriage of Jewish daughters and the laws of inheritance, see the Old Testament ruling in Numbers xxxvi: 6—12.

33 Compare *The Jew of Malta*, I. ii. 68ff. and *Merchant of Venice*, IV. i. 376. Marlowe is rebel enough to make Barabas call this Christian offer a sheer sin of theft against the Seventh Commandment and worse than his sin against the Eighth Commandment, 'covetousness'.

34 There is no reason to place much emphasis on this phrase since, technically, Antonio — being a Christian — was expected not to lend money at interest. If anything, the phrase shows how interrelated the two aspects of Shylock's case against Antonio were. See J. Russell Brown, ed., *The Merchant of Venice*, pp. xlii—v.

35 Cf. Hazlitt's comments on Kean's rendering of Shylock. Kean had substituted a sardonic intellect and fiery spirit for the malevolence of earlier actors; in the process, Hazlitt observed, Shylock became 'more than half a Christian. Certainly, our sympathies are much oftener with him than with his enemies. He is honest in his vices; they are hypocrites in their virtues.' Quoted by John Russell Brown, 'The Realization of Shylock: A Theatrical Criticism', *Early Shakespeare*, Stratford-Upon-Avon Studies, no. 3 (London, 1961) pp. 193—4.

36 J. Dover Wilson (ed.), *The Merchant of Venice* (Cambridge, 1953) p. xviii.

37 *Shakespeare's Politics*, p. 23. It is not really correct to say that 'revenge' is the only spiritual element in the list. Shylock does mention 'affections, passions'. In any case, as I point out later, the subject of his speech is revenge.

38 See also *The Merchant of Venice*, I. iii. 156—8.

39 Shylock would not eat Antonio's flesh for it is neither the 'fish' nor the 'flesh' approved of in the *Kashruth*. Shylock appreciates the implied insult in his reply: 'To bait fish withal.' Launcelot jokes in a similarly coarse vein in his conversation with Jessica in III. v: 'this making of Christians will raise the price of hogs, — if we grow all to be pork-eaters, we shall not shortly have a rasher on the coals for money.'

40 E.g., *Merchant*, I. iii. 173—5; II. ii. 106—8; II. iv. 34; II. vii. 51.

41 'The Merchant of Venice: The Gentle Bond', *ELH*, XXIX (Sep 1962), 240—1.

42 See the description of this rhetorical tradition in E. Auerbach, *Mimesis* (New York, 1953) p. 34.

43 A racial, not merely a personal whim, as it is taken to be in the case of Aaron in *Titus Andronicus*. See Eldred D. Jones, 'Aaron and Melancholy in *Titus Andronicus*' *SQ*, XIV (spring 1963), 178—9. It is interesting, in any case, considering the argument of this chapter, that Dr Johnson felt the answer was given gratuitously 'to aggravate the pain' of Shylock's adversaries.

44 Allan Bloom (p. 27) puts this bluntly: 'Portia goes off to Venice to save Antonio, not out of any principle of universal humanity, but because he is her husband's friend, and Bassanio is involved in the responsibility for his plight.'

45 Manya Lifschitz-Holden, *Les Juifs dans la Littérature Française du Moyen Age* (New York, 1935) pp. 130—1.

46 E.g., 'If thou dost shed One drop of Christian blood' (II. 305—6); 'or pay the bond thrice And let the Christian go' (II. 314—5). It should be noticed that *Il Pecorone* merely states: 'If you shed one drop of blood,' etc. (Bullough, p. 473); and that Shylock himself (in the second example) sees Antonio as 'the Christian' rather than as 'rival' or 'debtor'.

47 In several medieval miracle plays, the conversion of Jewish merchants was effected by some divine intervention, and for good reason. 'Le Juif converti sait faire un noble usage de sa fortune mal accumulée. 'Qui'il out pris e muscie uilment. Il partage ses biens et pratique pieusement la charité que la religion chrétienne prescrit, car il aime Marie.' In another example of a blaspheming Jewish merchant, the Saviour appears and says to him: 'Ne m'insulte pas ainsi, o juif! Je ne peux avoir d'obligation ni abandonner mon serviteur dans la souffrance; prends ce qui t'appartint'. Following this 'le juif se fit baptiser avec sa femme et tous les siens.' Lifschitz-Holden, pp. 129—30; 131.

48 But see Grebanier, p. 29; the demand was 'simply an act of

extraordinary kindness to bring the non-believer into the true faith.'

49 *The Decameron of Giovanni Boccaccio*, tr. John Payne (London, 1931) pp. 25, 28.

50 *Merchant*, V. i. 54—63; see J. Russell Brown (ed.), *The Merchant of Venice*, 'Introduction', p. xli, for a brief account of the interpretation of the character and tradition of Jessica.

51 *The Historie of the World* (London, 1914) p. 61.

52 Quoted in R. W. Battenhouse, *Marlowe's Tamburlaine*, (Nashville, 1941) p. 33.

53 *The Jew of Malta*, ed. H. S. Bennett (London, 1930) p. 19.

CHAPTER 3

1 All references to *Othello* are to the Arden edition by M. R. Ridley (London, 1958).

2 See W. E. Miller, 'Negroes in Elizabethan London', *N. & Q*, CCVI (1961) 138; Eldred D. Jones, 'African in Elizabethan England', *N & Q*, n.s., VIII (1961) 302, *Othello's Countrymen* (London, 1965) and *The Elizabethan Image of Africa* (Washington, 1971).

3 G. L. Kittredge (ed.), *The Tragedy of Othello* (Boston, 1936) p. xi. For a discussion of the preceding argument, see Philip Butcher, 'Othello's Racial Identity', *SQ*, III (1952) 243.

4 *Coleridge's Shakespearean Criticism*, ed. T. M. Raysor (Cambridge, Mass., 1930) I. p. 47.

5 Quoted in Ernest Zeisler, *Othello: Time Enigma and Color Problem* (Chicago, 1954) pp. 58—9.

6 Ibid., p. 59.

7 A. C. Bradley, *Shakespearean Tragedy* (London, 1905) p. 198; Chambers is quoted by J. Dover Wilson, in '*Titus Andronicus* on the Stage in 1595', *Shakespeare Survey*, I (1948) 21.

8 *The Masque of Blackness* (1605) in *Works*, eds. Herford and Simpson, VII (Oxford, 1941) p. 169.

9 W. E. Miller (1961) p. 158.

10 Philip Butcher (1952) p. 247.

11 J. Dover Wilson (ed.), *Othello* (Cambridge, 1951) pp. xi, ix—x, xii.

12 Ruth L. Anderson, *Elizabethan Psychology and Shakespeare's Plays*, University of Iowa Humanistic Studies, III, no. 4 (1927) 50ff. See also Eldred D. Jones, 'Aaron and Melancholy in *Titus Andronicus*', *SQ*, XIV (1963), 178—9, where the melancholy is shown to be associated in Elizabethan minds — at least in Burton's — with the 'hot countries'.

13 See R. V. Lindabury, *A Study of Patriotism in the Elizabethan Drama* (London, 1931) pp. 103—25.

14 Quoted by Lois Whitney, 'Did Shakespeare Know Leo Africanus?' *PMLA*, XXXVII (Sep 1922) 482.

15 R. R. Cawley, *The Voyagers and Elizabethan Drama* (Boston, 1958) pp. 349, 351.

16 Since the acceptance of black 'stage Othello', this view has been receiving more attention. Desmond MacCarthy (*New Statesman and Nation*, Apr 9, 1932, p. 451) complained of Ernest Milton's acting of Othello: 'What we are given . . . is a frail, tense Oriental, of apparently Hebrew rather than Moorish extraction, whom it seems more natural to imagine attaining eminence through brains and cunning than through a splendid virile audacity.' And according to Kenneth Tynan ('Olivier's Othello', *The Observer* Sunday Supplement, London, Dec 12, 1965, p. 12), Sir Laurence believed that the play 'belonged to Iago who could always make the Moor look a credulous idiot'. Sir Laurence, Tynan says, must have spoken 'with authority' since he 'had played Iago to Ralph Richardson's Othello in 1938'.

17 Dover Wilson, 'Introduction', *Othello* (1951) p. xii and Paul A. Jorgensen, ' "Perplex'd in the Extreme": The Role of Thought in *Othello*,' *SQ*, XV (1964) 269.

18 Discussed in Marvin Rosenberg, *The Masks of Othello* (Berkeley, 1961) p. 185.

19 In Samuel Purchas, *Purchas His Pilgrimes* (1625) V (Glasgow, 1905) p. 356.

20 Cf., e.g., Maud Bodkin, *Archetypal Patterns in Poetry* (New York, 1961) p. 211, where she attempts 'some study of the tragedy of *Othello* in order to examine the figure of Iago in relation to Othello, and to compare it with Mephistopheles in relation to Faust.' Othello is described (p. 214) as 'a symbol of faith in human values of love and war'.

21 *The Common Pursuit* (London, 1952) pp. 146—7.

22 *Odyssey*, I. 22—4; *Iliad*, XXIII. 205—7: *Odyssey*, IV. 84 and Iliad, I. 423—4. On the negro in Classical Art, see Grace M. Beardsley, *The Negro in Greek and Roman Civilization*, Johns Hopkins Studies in Archaeology, no. 4 (Baltimore, 1919) pp. 7—20.

23 *Lucan*, tr. J. D. Duff, Loeb edn. (London, 1928) IV. 684—6.

24 *Purchas His Pilgrimes*, V, p. 332.

25 Quoted by Lois Whitney (1922) p. 483.

26 See J. Milton French, 'Othello among the Anthropophagi', *PMLA*, XLIV (1934), 807—9, in which he cites maps of 1535 with details

such as Othello describes to the Senate. A 'Tabula Nova Partis Aphri', for example, shows men with one eye in their chests. Another, 'India Orientalis', represents men chopping bodies into small pieces convenient for cooking: 'His sunt antropophagi'.

27 Dover Wilson, *Othello* (1951) pp. xix, xx.

28 *Shakespeare and the Stoicism of Seneca* (London, 1927) p. 110.

29 'Diabolic Intellect and the Noble Hero' in *The Common Pursuit* (London, 1962) p. 152.

30 Barbara Everett, 'Reflections on the Sentimentalist's *Othello*', *The Critical Quarterly*, vol. 3, no. 2 (summer 1961) 132, 139, 138.

31 Lindabury (1931) p. 102.

32 Rev. Francis X. Gokey, *The Terminology for the Devil and Evil Spirits in the Apostolic Fathers*, Catholic University of America Patristic Studies, XCIII (Washington 1961) pp. 112–13, 127, 175.

33 Quoted in Welker Given, *A Further Study of the Othello*, Papers of the Shakespeare Society of New York, no. 11 (New York, 1899) p. 26.

34 *Mirror of the World* (ed.), Oliver H. Prior, Early English Text Society (Oxford 1931) pp. 66, 67, 94.

35 *Purchas His Pilgrimes*, IX, p. 216.

36 There is evidence that the Elizabethans regarded the blackman as a descendant of Ham. See, for example, *Purchas His Pilgrimes*, VIII, p. 585: 'from the Mountaynes of Chus, that is Ethiopia ... And these bee those blacke Slaves very well knowne to all, of the Posterities of Cham.' Raleigh (*Historie of the World*, London 1614, p. 132) makes the case for Phut, another son of Ham, instead of Chus, as the father of the African. Shakespeare does not refer to Ham, but he was certainly aware of the tradition because he does recognise Japheth in (*2 Henry IV*. II. ii. 129–30) as the father of Europe. There is an elaborate identification of Ham and the blackman in Rabbinical literature and this would certainly have been known to Elizabethan preachers and exegetes. A summary of this tradition is in L. Gizenberg, *The Legends of the Jews*, (New York, 1909) p. 108. Ham is associated with the blackman in Cowley's *Davideis*, Marvell's *Upon Appleton House*, and in Defoe's *A System of Magick*. According to Jewish legend, Ham was turned black, with the raven, after the Flood. Their sin was sexual intemperance.

37 S. L. Bethell, 'The Diabolic Images of *Othello*', *Shakespeare Survey*, VI (1952) 62–80; Paul N. Siegel, 'The Damnation of Othello', *PMLA*, LXVIII (1953) 1068–78. For a recent rebuttal of their argument, see Robert H. West, 'The Christianness of *Othello*', *SQ,*

XV (1964) 333—43.

38 Rymer, *A Short View of Tragedy* (1693), in *The Critical Works of Thomas Rymer*, ed. Curt Zimansky (New Haven, 1956) p. 160. Rymer thinks Shakespeare does this so that Othello 'might have a convenient while so to *roul his Eyes*, and so to *gnaw his nether* lip to the spectators.'

CHAPTER 4

1 Arthur O. Lovejoy, 'The Supposed Primitivism of Rousseau's *Discourse on Unequality*', and 'Monboddo and Rousseau' in *Essays in the History of Ideas* (Baltimore, 1948) pp. 14—61.

2 Lovejoy, 'Monboddo and Rousseau', in *Essays in the History of Ideas*, p. 57.

3 H. N. Fairchild, *The Noble Savage, A Study in Romantic Naturalism* (New York, 1928) and Wylie Sypher, *Guinea's Captive Kings* (Chapel Hill, 1942). Sypher (p. 107) argues that 'the increasingly defamatory reports of travellers do not seem to sober this primitivisitic level . . . there was, in truth, an incorrigible will to believe in the noble savage.'

4 See chapter 2 above.

5 James E. Phillips, '*The Tempest* and the Renaissance Idea of Man', *SQ*, XV (spring 1964) 150.

6 Ibid., p. 152.

7 John E. Hankins, 'Caliban, the Bestial Man', *PMLA*, LXII (Sep 1947) 793.

8 Walter Raleigh, *The Historie of the World* (London, 1614) p. 95.

9 No such conditioning was necessary for the realisation of the allegorical import of, for example, the fairy gods and goddesses of *A Midsummer Night's Dream*. There, because the fairies have a totally fictional and legendary existence, the audience does not have to have an attitude to them *as people*.

10 H. N. Fairchild (1928) p. 21.

11 Preserved Smith, *The Enlightenment, 1687—1776* (New York, 1962) p. 140.

12 Desiderius Erasmus, *The Praise of Folly*, tr. John Wilson in 1668, (Ann Arbor, 1958) p. 57.

13 Quoted in Louis I. Bredvold, *The Brave New World of the Enlightenment* (Ann Arbor, 1961) p. 60.

14 Quoted by A. O. Lovejoy, *Essays in the History of Ideas* (Balti-

more, 1948) pp. 16, 19.

15 D. Defoe, *Robinson Crusoe* (New York, 1941) p. 199.

16 H. N. Fairchild, p. 53.

17 In *The Works of Aphra Behn*, ed. Montague Summers (London, 1915) vol. V, p. 133.

18 *Robinson Crusoe*, p. 161.

19 Thomas Southern, *Oroonoko, A Tragedy in New British Theatre*, vol. VI (London, 1776) p. 34. Since this edition does not number lines and scenes, page references have been given to facilitate reference.

20 Ibid., p. 17.

21 *The Works of Aphra Behn*, p. 170.

22 H. N. Fairchild, (1928) p. 170.

23 W. Sypher, (1942) pp. 261, 264.

24 *Robinson Crusoe*, p. 22.

25 Ibid., p. 192.

26 Ibid., p. 193.

27 Ibid., pp. 194—5.

28 Ibid., p. 197.

29 Ibid., p. 200.

30 Ibid., p. 202.

31 According to R. R. Cawley, *The Voyagers and Elizabethan Drama* (Boston, 1938) p. 338, it was widely held in Elizabethan times that the Indians thought Europeans to be gods.

32 *Robinson Crusoe*, pp. 202—3.

33 *Oroonoko*, p. 164.

34 Ibid., p. 166.

35 *Oroonoko*, p. 60.

36 Monboddo, *Origin and Progress of Language*, 2nd ed. (1789) vol. I, p. 262; quoted in Lovejoy, (1948) p. 53.

37 Memoirs of Richard Cumberland, *Written by Himself with Illustrative Notes by Henry Flanders* (Philadelphia, 1856) pp. 141—2.

38 Edgar Rosenberg, *From Shylock to Svengali* (Stanford, 1960) p. 39.

39 Rosenberg, p. 48.

40 Ibid., p. 39.

CHAPTER 5

1 *Travels in the Congo*, tr. Dorothy Bussy (Los Angeles, 1962) p. 13.

2 Ibid., p. 14.

3 Ibid., p. 14.
4 Ibid., pp. 4, 5, 7; 266.
5 Ibid., p. 4.
6 Neville H. Newhouse, *Joseph Conrad* (London, 1966) p. 39.
7 Quoted in Newhouse (1966) p. 39.
8 Ian Watt, 'Conrad Criticism and *The Nigger of the "Narcissus"*', *Nineteenth Century Fiction*, XII (1958) 257—83. Subsequent references to this article are given in parentheses.
9 J. E. Miller Jr, '*The Nigger of the "Narcissus"*: A Re-examination,' *PMLA*, LXVI (1951) 911—18; Vernon Young, 'Trial by Water: Joseph Conrad's *The Nigger of the "Narcissus"*', *Accent*, XII (1952) 67—81. See also W. R. Martin, 'The Captain of the *"Narcissus"*', *English Studies in Africa*, VI (1963) 191—7.
10 'Symbolism in *The Nigger of the "Narcissus"*', *TCL*, II (1956) 29.
11 A term that also includes the other term 'white'.
12 Hermann Melville, *Moby Dick*, ed. Alfred Kazin (Boston, 1956) p. 37.
13 F. J. Masback, 'Conrad's Jonahs', *College English*, XXII (1961) 332.
14 H. E. Davis, 'Symbolism in *The Nigger of the "Narcissus"*', p. 26.
15 *The Shadow Line: A Confession* (New York, 1917) p. 91.
16 Melville, *Redburn, His First Voyage* (New York, 1957) p. 55.
17 *The Nigger of the 'Narcissus'* (London, 1955). All subsequent references are to this edition and will be given in parentheses after quotations.
18 Cf. Melville, *Moby Dick*, p. 58:
    Savage though Queequeg was, and hideously marred about the face — at least to my taste — his countenance yet had a something in it which was by no means disagreeable. You cannot hide the soul. Through all his unearthly tattooings, I thought I saw traces of a simple honest heart ... Queequeg was George Washington cannibalistically developed.

19 *Tales of Hearsay* (New York, 1925).

Bibliography

A: BOOKS

Alvarez, A., *Stewards of Excellence: Studies in Modern English and American Poets* (New York, 1958).

Anderson, Ruth L., *Elizabethan Psychology and Shakespeare's Plays* (Des Moines, 1927).

Auerbach, E., *Mimesis* (New York, 1953).

Battenhouse, R. W., *Marlowe's 'Tamburlaine'* (Nashville, 1941).

Beardesley, Grace M., *The Negro in Greek and Roman Civilization* (Baltimore, 1919).

Bennett, H. S. (ed.), *The Jew of Malta* (London, 1930).

Bloom, Allan, *Shakespeare's Politics* (New York, 1964).

Bodkin, Maud, *Archetypal Patterns in Poetry* (New York, 1961).

Bradley, A. C., *Shakespearean Tragedy* (London, 1905).

Bredvold, Louis I., *The Brave New World of the Enlightenment* (Ann Arbor, 1961).

Brooks, Cleanth, *William Faulkner: The Yoknapatawpha Country* (New Haven, 1963).

Bullough, Geoffrey, *Narrative and Dramatic Sources of Shakespeare*, vol. 1 (London, 1957).

Casey, John, *The Language of Criticism* (London, 1966).

Cawley, R. R., *The Voyagers and Elizabethan Drama* (Boston, 1938).

Charlton, H. B., *Shakespearean Comedy* (London, 1949).

Conrad, J., *The Nigger of the 'Narcissus'* (London, 1955).

Conrad, J., *The Shadow Line: A Confession* (New York, 1917).

Conrad, J., *Tales of Hearsay* (New York, 1925).

Cowley, Malcolm (ed.), *The Portable Faulkner* (New York, 1954).

Culler, Jonathan, *Structuralist Poetics: Structuralism, Linguistics and the Study of Literature* (London, 1975).

Cumberland, Richard, *Memoirs of Richard Cumberland ... with Illustrative Notes by Henry Flanders* (Philadelphia, 1856).

Defoe, Daniel, *Robinson Crusoe* (New York, 1941).

Dover Wilson, J. (ed.), *The Merchant of Venice* (Cambridge, 1953).

Duff, J. D. (tr.), *Lucan* (London, 1928).

Duthie, George I., *Shakespeare* (London, 1951).

Eliot, T. S., *Shakespeare and the Stoicism of Seneca* (London, 1927).

Erasmus, Desiderius, *The Praise of Folly*, tr. John Wilson (Ann Arbor, 1958).

Fairchild, H. N., *The Noble Savage: A Study in Romantic Naturalism* (New York, 1928).

Faulkner, William, *Go Down, Moses* (New York, 1942).

Faulkner, William, *Light in August* (London, 1973).

Fisch, H., *The Dual Image: A Study of the Figure of the Jew in English Literature* (London, 1959).

Friedlander, G., *Shakespeare and the Jew* (London, 1921).

Gide, André, *Travels in the Congo*, tr. Dorothy Bussy (Los Angeles, 1962).

Ginzberg, L., *The Legends of the Jews* (New York, 1909).

Given, Welker, *A Further Study of 'Othello'* (New York, 1899).

Gokey, Rev. Francis X., *The Terminology for the Devil and Evil Spirits in the Apostolic Fathers* (Washington, D.C., 1961).

Grebanier, B., *The Truth About Shylock* (New York, 1959).

Guiraud, P., *Semiology*, tr. George Gross (London, 1975).

Gwynn, Frederick L. and Joseph L. Blotner, *Faulkner in the University* (Charlottesville, 1959).

Hackforth, R. (tr.), *Plato's Phaedrus* (Cambridge, 1952).

Herford, C. H. and P. and E. Simpson, (eds.), *Ben Jonson: Works*, vols VII, X (London, 1941, 1950).

Howe, Irving, *William Faulkner: A Critical Study* (New York, 1962).

Hume, David, *Treatise of Human Nature*, Bk I (New York, 1962).

Jones, E. D., *The Elizabethan Image of Africa* (Washington, D.C., 1971).

Jones, E. D., *Othello's Countrymen* (London, 1965).

Keynes, G. (ed.), *Complete Writings of William Blake* (London, 1966).

Kittredge, G. L. (ed.), *The Tragedy of Othello* (Boston, 1936).

Leavis, F. R., *The Common Pursuit* (London, 1952).

Leavis, F. R., *The Living Principle: English as a Discipline of Thought* (London, 1975).

Lifschiz-Holden, Manya, *Les Juifs dans la littérature Française du Moyen Age* (New York, 1935).

Lindabury, R. V., *A Study of Patriotism in the Elizabethan Drama* (London, 1931).

Longley Jr, John L., *The Tragic Mask: A Study of Faulkner's Heroes* (Chapel Hill, 1963).

Lovejoy, Arthur O., *Essays in the History of Ideas* (Baltimore, 1948).

Melville, H., *Redburn, His First Voyage* (New York, 1957).

Melville, H., *Moby Dick*, ed. Alfred Kazin (Boston, 1956).

Middleton Murry, J., *The Problem of Style* (Oxford, 1922).

Millett, Fred B. and Bentley, Gerald E., *The Art of the Drama* (New York, 1935).

Minter, David L., *Twentieth Century Interpretations of 'Light in August'*, (Englewood Cliffs, N.J., 1969).

Nelson, B. N., *The Ideas of Usury* (Princeton, 1949).

Newhouse, Neville H., *Joseph Conrad* (London, 1966).

Ortolan, J. L. E., *The History of Roman Law* (London, 1871).

Payne, John (tr.), *The Decameron of Giovanni Boccaccio* (London, 1931).

Pollard, A. W., *English Miracle Plays* (Oxford, 1909).

Prior, Oliver H. (ed.), *Mirror of the World* (Oxford, 1931).

Purchas, Samuel, *Purchas His Pilgrimes* (1625), vol. V (Glasgow, 1905).

Raleigh, Sir Walter, *The Historie of the World* (1614) (London, 1914).

Raysor, T. M. (ed.), *Coleridge's Shakespearean Criticism* (Cambridge, Mass., 1930).

Ridley, M. R. (ed.), *Othello* (London, 1958).

Rosenberg, Edgar, *From Shylock to Svengali: Jewish Stereotypes in English Literature* (Stanford, 1960).

Russell Brown, J. (ed.), *The Merchant of Venice* (London, 1955).

Schorer, Mark (ed.), *Sinclair Lewis: A Collection of Critical Essays* (Englewood Cliffs, N.J., 1962).

Smith, Preserved, *The Enlightenment 1687–1776* (New York, 1962).

Stevens, Wallace, *Collected Poems* (New York, 1954).

Summers, Montague, (ed.), *The Works of Aphra Behn* (London, 1915).

Sypher, Wylie (ed.), *Enlightened England: An Anthology of English Literature from Dryden to Blake* (New York, 1962).

Sypher, Wylie, *Guinea's Captive Kings* (Chapel Hill, 1942).

Wager, Willis, *American Literature: A World View* (London, 1969).

Whitney, Lois, *Primitivism and the Idea of Progress* (New York, 1934).

Wilson, Mona (ed.), *Johnson: Prose and Poetry* (London, 1957).

Zeisler, E., *Othello: Time Enigma and Color Problem* (Chicago, 1954).

Zimansky, Curt (ed.), *The Critical Works of Thomas Rhymer* (New Haven, 1956).

B: ARTICLES

Bethell, S. L., 'The Diabolic Images of *Othello*', *Shakespeare Survey*, VI (1952).

Brown, Beatrice D., 'Medieval Prototypes of Lorenzo and Jessica', *MLN*, XLIV (1929).

Davis, Harold E., 'Symbolism in *The Nigger of the "Narcissus"*,' *TCL*, II (1956).

Eberly, Ralph D., 'Blake's "Little Black Boy",' *Explicator*, XV (Apr 1957).

Elder, Doris L., 'The Meaning of Wallace Steven's Two Themes', *Critical Quarterly*, II, no. 2 (summer 1969).

Everett, Barbara, 'Reflections on the Sentimentalist's Othello', *The Critical Quarterly*, III, no. 2 (summer 1961).

French, J. Milton, 'Othello Among the Anthropophagi', *PMLA*, XLIV (1934).

Hankins, John E., 'Caliban, the Bestial Man', *PMLA*, LXII (Sep 1947).

Jones, Eldred D., 'Aaron and Melanchology in *Titus Andronicus*', *SQ*, XIV (spring 1963).

Jones, Eldred D., 'Africans in Elizabethan England', *N & Q*, VIII (1961).

Jorgensen, A., ' "Perplex'd in the Extreme": The Role of Thought in *Othello*', *SQ*, XV (1964).

Martin, W. R., 'The Captain of the *"Narcissus"*,' *English Studies in Africa*, VI (1963).

Masback, F. J., 'Conrad's Jonahs', *College English*, XXII (1961).

Miller, J. E., Jr, *'The Nigger of the "Narcissus"*: A Re-examination', *PMLA* (1951).

Miller, W. E., 'Negroes in Elizabethan London', *N & Q*, CCVI (1961).

Nathan, Norman, 'Shylock, Jacob and God's Judgment', *SQ*, I (Oct 1950).

Phillips, James E., *'The Tempest* and the Renaissance *Idea of Man*', *SQ*, XV (spring 1964).

Ribner, Irving, 'Marlowe and Shakespeare', *SQ*, XV (spring 1964).

Russell Brown, J., 'The Realization of Shylock: A Theatrical Criticism', *Early Shakespeare* (Stratford-Upon-Avon Studies, no. 3; London, 1961).

Schwartz, Delmore, 'The Ultimate Plato with Picasso's Guitar', *Harvard Advocate*, CXXVII (Dec 1940).

Siegel, Paul N., 'The Damnation of Othello', *PMLA*, LXVIII (1953).

Tynan, Kenneth, 'Olivier's Othello', *The (London) Observer* Supplement, 12 Dec 1965.

Watt, Ian, 'Conrad Criticism and *The Nigger of the "Narcissus"*,' *Nineteenth Century Fiction*, XII (1958).

West, Robert H., 'The Christianness of Othello', *SQ*, XV (1964).

Whitesell, J. Edwin, 'Blake's "Little Black Boy",' *Explicator*, V (Apr 1947).

Whitney, Lois, 'Did Shakespeare Know Leo Africanus?' *PMLA*, XXXVII (Sep 1922).

Wilkins, Leah W., 'Shylock's Pound of Flesh and Laban's Sheep', *MLN*, LVII (1947).

Young, Vernon, 'Trial by Water: Joseph Conrad's *The Nigger of the "Narcissus"*,' *Accent*, XII (1952).

Index